Praise for *Pause Br...*

"Both simple and profound, practical and inspiring, humorous and heart-opening, immediately useful and thoroughly comprehensive. Reading it feels like being with a wise old Zen master twinkling with the eyes of a young child. Such a sweet, wonderful book."

RICK HANSON, PHD
author of the *New York Times* bestselling *Buddha's Brain*,
Hardwiring Happiness, and *Resilient: How to Grow an Unshakable Core of Calm, Strength, and Happiness*

"A readable version of plain, sane goodness."
AL YOUNG
California Poet Laureate, author of *Drowning in the Sea of Love*

"Such a delightful approach to everyday mindfulness!"
SHARON SALZBERG
author of *Real Happiness*

"This book goes beyond anything I expected. It opened doors to simple, actionable practices that left me smiling for days while exposing deeper truths of the energy beneath. Gary's unique prose pierces through the common layers of anxious spin, bringing me to a verdant vista of perspective and peace. I dare anyone not to widen their eyes with wonder."
SEAN FARGO
founder of MindfulnessExercises.com

"After studying and practicing the teachings of Thich Nhat Hanh for years, I found his essence creatively offered in this book."
JERRY BRAZA, PHD
author of Seeds of Love *and* Moment by Moment

"A lovely offering of wisdom, practices, and kindness to help foster a mindful life and a compassionate heart."

JACK KORNFIELD
author of *No Time Like the Present*

"Clear and inviting, [this book is] perfect for beginners but also wonderful for more experienced practitioners looking for a refreshing review. A deeply enjoyable and inspiring read."

YAEL SHY
author of *What Now? Meditation for Your Twenties and Beyond*

"Gary Gach offers us a sweet, often humorous, and always engaging presentation of an ancient spiritual discipline. *Pause Breathe Smile* gives us mindfulness as a universalist spiritual discipline. I recommend it."

JAMES ISHMAEL FORD
author of *If You're Lucky, Your Heart Will Break* and *Zen Master Who?*

"A delightful book! Gary Gach's writing is wise, practical, playful, and encouraging. My mindfulness practice was reinvigorated and deepened in surprising ways as a result of Gary's insights. Highly recommended!"

DANIEL P. COLEMAN
author of *Presence and Process: A Path Toward Transformative Faith and Inclusive Community*

"Stress at work? A technical meltdown? Having a bad day? Having a good day? Don't know what to do today? Start with poet Gary Gach's simple formula for returning to sanity and grace. What a fine and much-needed book, especially now. A lifetime of practice is folded into this elegant book. It is guaranteed to make you smile."

PATRICIA RYAN MADSON
author of *Improv Wisdom*

"Gary Gach's life is his art. Reading this book will make you feel younger, wiser, and more fully yourself." TIM DESMOND
author of *Self-Compassion in Psychotherapy* and
Staying Human in a F*cked Up World

"So simple! So skillful! So necessary! Bravo to Gary Gach for penning this brilliant approach to mindfulness for all of us. I will be using it in my yoga and meditation classes, and taking its wisdom to heart in my own life and practice."
LEZA LOWITZ
author of *Yoga Poems, Up from the Sea*, and *Sacred Sanskrit Words*

"Gach's words are wise and go down easy, and his voice is as sweet and clear as the mindfulness bell itself. DELIGHTFUL."
WES NISKER
author of *You Are Not Your Fault; Buddha's Nature;* and
The Big Bang, The Buddha, and the Baby Boom

"*Pause Breathe Smile* is an invitation to witness, enjoy, and engage the wonders of life. Gach reveals how we can get in touch with our True Nature. Mindfulness does not need to be an intermittent part of our life. It is available to us every moment!" RICH LEWIS
author of *Centering Prayer Journey*

"A mindfulness manual, a twenty-first century theology, and especially a cure for most kinds of anxiety. Gach takes us literally beyond religion to gratitude, joy, and sanctity. Gach's world is one filled with an all-pervading holiness and taking responsibility for one's life. It is neither meditation nor religion but 'present-ness,' which we suspect is the goal of both."
RABBI LAWRENCE KUSHNER
author of *Eyes Remade for Wonder, The Book of Letters,*
The Book of Words, and *Kaballah: A Love Story*

also from gary gach

AS AUTHOR

The Complete Idiot's Guide to Understanding Buddhism

*Writers.net: Every Writer's Guide to Essential Resources
and Opportunities*

*Pocket Guide to the Internet: The No-Sweat Guide
to the Information Superhighway*

Preparing the Ground: Poems 1960–1970

AS EDITOR

What Book!?: Buddha Poems from Beat to Hiphop

AS TRANSLATOR OF KO UN,
with Brother Anthony of Taizé and Young-Moo Kim

Flowers of a Moment

Songs for Tomorrow

Ten Thousand Lives

pause breathe smile

awakening mindfulness
when meditation is not enough

Gary Gach

SOUNDS TRUE
BOULDER, COLORADO

Sounds True
Boulder, CO 80306

Published 2018

Cover design by Rachael Murray
Book design by Beth Skelley

Cover image (calligraphy) by Denise L. Nguyen

Printed in Canada

Library of Congress Cataloging-in-Publication Data

Names: Gach, Gary, author.
Title: Pause breathe smile : awakening mindfulness when meditation
  is not enough / Gary Gach.
Description: Boulder, Colorado : Sounds True, 2018.
Identifiers: LCCN 2017061605 (print) | LCCN 2018009672 (ebook) |
  ISBN 9781683642077 (ebook) | ISBN 9781683641759 (pbk.)
Subjects: LCSH: Ānāpānasmṛti. | Respiration—Religious
  aspects—Buddhism.
Classification: LCC BQ5630.A6 (ebook) | LCC BQ5630.A6 G33 2018
  (print) | DDC 294.3/443—dc23
LC record available at https://lccn.loc.gov/2017061605

10 9 8 7 6 5 4 3 2 1

To Chau Yoder,
for tending the PBS hearth before me

To Lyn Fine,
for mindful peacebuilding

To Sister Chan Khong,
just because

To Thay,
thank you for your life

Mindfulness is something soft, quiet, gentle, and discreet, but nevertheless it has the capacity to embrace all aspects of our life. It imbues every pore of our skin and every part of our being. When we're aware of our breathing, our steps, or a drop of dew that is hanging from the tip of a leaf, that awareness is gentle and soft like the moonlight. Yet it's ever penetrating and it brings a certain quality of brightness and lightness to us. We feel connected to that dewdrop, to that leaf, to that in-breath and out-breath, and to every aspect of our life. Quietly and slowly, we feel connected to life itself.

SISTER DANG NGHIEM

Contents at a Glance

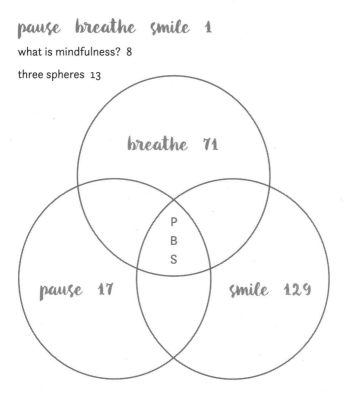

pause breathe smile 1

smile

END COMMENTARY

pause breathe smile 187

pause breathe smile

WHEN I'M ASKED BY STRANGERS, "What do you *do*?" I could reply that I write books, swim in the San Francisco Bay, and love creativity in myriad forms. Yet, more often than not, I'm sincerely stumped for words. Honestly. I'm inexpressibly grateful to have a grounding in my life from which everything grows.

Call it "Zen." Call it "mindfulness." Call it a "path of awakening." These are just convenient labels for the one thing needful, which gives my life solidity and direction, meaning and joy. Labels are good for cans, not people. So, just as I do with perfect strangers, rather than talk about it, I invite you to please join with me, right now, for three "mindful" breaths, so we can see for ourselves together . . . directly experiencing what it is I "do."

But before we do, here are three points to keep in mind:

1 We're not changing our breathing, we're just being aware of it.

2 We'll count the cycle of an in-breath and out-breath as one breath.

3 We'll breathe through our nostrils.

(Obviously, I can't talk and breathe at the same time, but I'll record here what I'm experiencing, what's going through my mind, as we do this together.)

Ready . . . set . . . *go!*

Breathing in . . . right now, I feel the air's freshness in my nostrils.

Breathing out . . . I sense my breath warm from being inside my body . . . *Ahhh!*

Was that nice? That's our breath number one. Let's enjoy another. This time, let's notice what else is going on.

Breathing in . . . I'm noticing I'm more aware of sounds, nearby and far off . . . how this breath's a bit deeper and slower . . . and how I'm more aware of my body this time . . . feeling my ribs moving, my posture lengthening a bit . . .

Breathing out . . . my whole body is settling downward, anchoring, grounding, toward Mother Earth.

Mmmmm, this is good!

One more time.

Breathing in . . . I feel more space, *spaciousness*,
   within and without.
Breathing out . . . I feel myself letting go completely.

This is very good indeed. So now (please, don't stop
being aware of your breathing), as a special treat, let's give
ourselves a gift . . . the gift of a half-smile. Join me as I lift
just one side of my mouth, in a wee, faint, itsy-bitsy half-
smile. (For me, Mona Lisa comes to mind, or the Buddha.)
Concentrating on this gentle half-smile, I relax all the other
muscles of my face. Breathing in and contacting any tension in my body and feelings and mind and then breathing
out and letting it all go. Completely *r e l e a s i n g*.

Breathing in.

Breathing out.

Mmmm . . . how nourishing breath is! I can feel the
oxygen refreshing every cell of my body, like a drink of
fresh cool water on a hot dusty trail. And doesn't breathing with just an itsy-bitsy, faint, Buddha half-smile *feel*
happier? (Nothing wrong with that.) Why meditate if
you don't enjoy it?

That's it, in a nutshell. This focused, friendly awareness,
and its spaciousness . . . stability . . . tranquility . . . happiness . . . are always available. You can tap in to it any time.
This awareness has no beginning, middle, nor end.

This experience is beyond words.

[*all the rest is commentary*]

COMMENTARY

LET OUR TITLE BE YOUR GUIDE. *Pause Breathe Smile*
(PBS) is an invitation you can always remember and
practice anytime, anywhere. Even right now. It's also the
outline for this manual of awakening mindfulness. But
flexibly so. Please use your creativity and intuition to
explore and play with pausing, breathing, and smiling,
and discover their varied dimensions for yourself.

In the front third of this book, I introduce a key
component of mindfulness not to be skimmed over.
Call it moral values in action. Such intentional, conscious conduct is meditation too. It's crucially needed
in the world we share. However, it doesn't just fall from
the skies. We need to awaken it within ourselves before
we can offer it to others too. Then, at the center of the
book are teachings on full awareness, with breath as a
natural guide. In the back third, I survey three elemental aspects of the Great Way of Reality, for opening
your wisdom eye.

Pause Breathe Smile's three parts are like booklets that
can be read in any order. (I insist on your freedom.) As
they come together in your one, unrepeatable, precious
life, they can interconnect as a marvelous, integral whole.

The time is ripe. Forty years ago, Vietnamese Zen
master Thich Nhat Hanh* published a book that helped
establish *mindfulness* in our contemporary vocabulary:
*The Miracle of Mindfulness: An Introduction to the Practice
of Meditation.* (The original manuscript title, by the way,
was *The Miracle of Awakening.*) Since then, mindfulness
has become the fastest-growing self-help trend of our

time since yoga. As mindfulness continues to evolve in the West, I hope this simple, threefold approach to its complete scope might help deepen and extend its meaning and potential. It is my experience that anyone can engage it in their lives as a healing and transformative practice, as they wish.

As with a cookbook, this book is not meant to be just read, it's to be performed, tried out, played with. If you're relatively new to mindfulness, here are various recipes for a nourishing, wholesome diet. If you've already danced with it a bit, this simple handbook offers a comprehensive view, as a top-level reference, with a few possible additions to your repertoire. And old hands might enjoy seeing already familiar basics in possibly new ways.

For me, it's been a mindfulness practice to stay happily aware of my breathing, and my environment, while writing one word after another, in an extended, anonymous love letter. Letter by letter. Breath by breath. And noticing the spaces in between.

My inmost wish is for these words to water your own, innate seeds of awakening.

Words can really only point you toward thresholds. How to go through them is up to you. A thousand-mile journey begins with just one step.

Enjoy the path.

---

*The English pronunciation is "Tik N'yat Hawn." However, since Vietnamese is a tonal language, this is only a close approximation for how one would pronounce it in Vietnamese. By his students worldwide he is affectionately known as Thay (pronounced "Tay" or "Tie").

what is mindfulness?

A rose by any other name would smell as sweet.

SHAKESPEARE

Revolutions don't necessarily follow in the wake of explosions and bloodshed. Sometimes they arrive as if on the paws of kittens. The revolution in consciousness that is mindfulness is one such example. And it's part of other historical contexts, such as the expansion of fitness to include wellness. It also takes place within an unnamed, contemplative movement in which people

are making the sacred real for themselves in daily life, beyond synagogues, pews, and prayer mats.

But what is mindfulness?

An elemental definition of mindfulness is that it's awareness.
— Look deeper.
British meditation teacher Bodhipaksa tells us:

> Mindfulness is the gentle effort to be
> continuously present with experience.

This echoes the Chinese word for mindfulness (念, *niàn*), which is the symbol for "this" or "now," over the symbol for "heart."* Having a heart fully in the present.

Here's another answer. Jon Kabat-Zinn has been at the forefront of the widespread acceptance, adoption, and articulation of mindfulness in the West. His basic, well-seasoned definition is so nuanced it can be broken out into bullet points. He says:

> Mindfulness means paying attention in a
> particular way:
>
>> on purpose,
>> in the present moment, and
>> nonjudgmentally.

---

*Look closely at the bottom half of the Chinese word, and you can see "heart" depicted as an actual heart, with its sac, auricle, and ventricle. It's very interesting to note too that this word for "heart" in Chinese also means "mind" — body and mind as one. A nondualist worldview is thus embedded within the language.

These three aspects neatly match up with PBS: on purpose (pausing), present moment (breathing), and non-judgmental (smiling).

When I'm asked to define mindfulness, at a party, or waiting for a bus — besides inviting the questioner to join me in pausing, breathing, smiling — I might say it is

> the energy of awakening . . . a state of intelligent alertness, open awareness with a kindly attitude, plus a gentle curiosity.

Maia Duerr is a cultural anthropologist and longtime practitioner. She has a somewhat different, brief definition:

> Mindfulness gives us a chance to listen to the wisdom of our hearts and to notice with more clarity where we get in our own way.

That's an equally viable, pith observation about mindfulness. And Vietnamese senior teacher Chan Khong puts it in yet another way. She once told an interviewer:

> Mindfulness is being still. It is profundity. You can look deeply right to the bottom of any situation . . . and know what needs to be done.

In that, I hear meditation (being still), wisdom (profundity), and intention (what needs to be done); all three, in one seamless stroke. I also hear the silent beat of the twin wings of mindfulness: the calm *stability* born of being still, which, in turn, enables insightful *looking deeply* into the present moment, to be in touch with whatever is called for.

Mindfulness can also be described as presence of mind; intelligent alertness; watchfulness; wakefulness; attentiveness to whatever's present; kindfulness; living in an enlightened, flourishing way.

That's the gist of it. All the rest is how you put it into *practice*. Pave your own way. Let it develop organically and, one day, you might offer a perfect stranger your own, active definition of mindfulness.

SPIRITUAL OR SECULAR: A COMMON REVERENCE FOR LIFE

Thomas Jefferson believed in "a wall of separation between church and state," and Americans today enjoy a presumably secular society. Yet the border between religion and secularism isn't always clear. I sometimes think of psychology and philosophy as secularizations of religion and theology. And see where we worship — look at how much reverence in our society is devoted, for example, to the Oscars and the Super Bowl. But an awakened view isn't dualist. As the word "*non-*secular" implies, secular and nonsecular reflect upon each other. Neither exists in a vacuum. So I keep to a middle path.

I mention all this because mindfulness is often treated now as a secular version of what are ancient traditions and lineages extending back to the time of the Buddha and before. With contemporary science as a bridge, secularization has enabled mindfulness to become accessible to millions. It has also made the contemplative, introspective, psychological dimensions of the tradition quite popular. This mainstream acceptance paves the way for me to present mindfulness as maybe more than a meditative technique, as something that can also offer active insight (wisdom) and relational values (ethics) in one well-rounded whole.

Mindfulness extends 360° to encompass the secular and religious alike. For instance, Phap De ("fap day"), a dear friend of mine, a former Gregorian monk, likens meditation to resting in Grace, and the energy of mindfulness to the Holy Spirit. For some, that view might be just the ticket. Mindfulness can complement any religious path, watering and deepening roots and extending wingspan by at least a few feathers. Or, if you're spiritual but nonreligious, it can be a perfect fit here too — there's nothing to bow down to or convert to. And mindfulness isn't altered one iota by belief or nonbelief in a creator deity or an afterlife, either way, so it's quite compatible with those who say, "Thank God I'm an atheist!"

three spheres

Mindfulness is a way of going about the business of living. PBS provides a recipe for the whole, traditional mindfulness pizza. It consists of just three basic ingredients with which you can concoct your own practice:

> Intentional, conscious conduct for a healthy lifestyle (pausing)
>
> Introspection and contemplation to calm and keep it real (breathing)
>
> Insight and clarity for a harmonious worldview (smiling)

Add extra toppings, according to taste, along with your own special seasonings and spices. "Taste and see" (Psalm 34:8).

There's no preset progression for PBS, like 1-2-3. Each phase is complete in and of itself, and the three phases also interconnect, providing positive feedback for each other. For example, insight awakens us (smiling) so we see a bigger picture beyond our limited views. We're not wishing things to be different from how they are, only to bump up against reality, over and over. An accurate worldview permits us to live in harmony with What Is.

Three interconnected spheres form a single map
of awakening mindfulness.

A worthy worldview needs to be put into action. At the root of such action is intention (pausing). Sound intention inclines us toward what's nourishing and leads away from what's harmful. We see how good it is to be in right relationship to ourselves and the world.

Insight opens our eyes to What Is. Intention brings us into harmony with How It Is. Together, they support a practice of silent, intuitive contemplation of reality and possibility (with calm, conscious breathing).

Such introspection can sober our mind, soften our heart, and awaken our soul. Space opens up for us. Here we can see our intentions and insights mirroring our mind-heart for us to investigate. Our practice has room to grow, as we continually learn in the light of our actual experience. More and more, we realize our true nature and become who we are meant to be. To realize and enjoy all this fully, ideally, we need the integral interaction of all three phases.

contemplation

lifestyle

worldview

pause

WHAT'S HAPPENING? PAUSE AND LOOK AROUND.
Addiction, political scandal, economic crime, environmental degradation, sexual slavery, teen suicide, ethnic cleansing, radical poverty, mindless violence, and the list goes on. One might think our world is devoid of moral values. Yet we all know what moral values are; putting them into action is where we can use further training. Such ethical training is integral to an awakened way of living, a mindful lifestyle. And learning to pause is at its heart.

Pause and look within. Is our goal in life only to satisfy our immediate desires? Is it all just entertainment? Are we here only to cultivate an image? Are we only sleepwalking through it all, or are we awake? Many of us have at least tasted our capacity for dignity and beauty, our ability to be totally aligned with our highest potential. But glimpses come and go. For them to become commonplace, we need to learn self-discipline. And we can master that well — through pausing.

This isn't rocket science. When we take a conscious breath, we're already pausing. And we're grounding ourselves in the here and now. We can listen to our heart, and set clear intentions. Considering the potential impact of our thoughts, our words, our deeds, we might choose inhibition or direction. The door is always open. It's up to us. With a smile, breathing easy, we get better at being human. We become good people. The universe opens up in silent applause when we take the leap to learn to pause.

discipline and mastery, growth and freedom

> Between stimulus and response there is a space.
> In that space is our power to choose our response.
> In our response lies our growth and our freedom.
> UNKNOWN (commonly misattributed to Viktor Frankl)

Pausing opens up space, within. Given space, we can incline toward intentionality, an intention-based lifestyle, establishing how we want to live in the world. Here are four practical avenues for bringing intentionality to any lifestyle:

1 Mindfulness bells
2 Mindfulness blessings
3 Mindfulness trainings
4 Studying. Observing. Practicing.

Mindfulness bells train us to pause, breathe, and calm, letting go of all else. Following an introduction to that marvelous discipline, we'll consider our moral perspective and intentionality. That will, in turn, lead us to mindfulness blessings. These are innovative ways to pause and set intention throughout our everyday lives. Then, we turn toward broader mindfulness trainings. We'll explore five bedrock trainings that can add indispensable relationality and responsibility to our lifestyle. In time, their guidelines can be seen not as a constraint of our heart but, rather, as a platform for our freedom.

In addition, I'll open up a game-changing view of motivation, then share a dynamic strategy for incorporating mindfulness trainings into daily life so you may continually grow and thrive. It's a method that can be equally applied to meditation and insight as well as conduct. All in all, these various forms of pausing nurture a space of growth and freedom, for our benefit and that of those close to us.

mindfulness bells

> Bells break in on our cares in order to remind us that all things pass away and that our preoccupations are not important. They speak to us of our freedom.
>
> THOMAS MERTON

If you visit a mindfulness retreat center in the Plum Village tradition of Thich Nhat Hanh, you'll discover handwritten signs along the road, in the parking lot, at a trailhead, or around a bend. A speed bump may be marked with a handwritten sign such as "Mindful Bump" or "Stop and Breathe." A plank hung up on a tree trunk may be engraved with calligraphy that reads, "Breathe, you are alive" or "Enjoy breathing." And visitors grow accustomed to the bells that announce the dawn chant, a morning talk, meals, and other daily events. Bells often find any of us reviewing the past or rehearsing the future, even if by only a few moments. When we hear a mindfulness bell, we relax, stop, and return to our conscious breathing. We consider the sound of a bell as the voice of the present moment reminding us to return to our true home in the here and now.

Thanks to mindfulness bell practice, learning to pause has become a daily habit for me. When I hear a bell, I stop what I'm saying, thinking, or doing. I let my muscles and nerves totally relax. I pay full attention to my in-breath and out-breath. I smile and simply *be*. Nothing else. (Instant nirvana.) Being mindful of three breaths can restore me to a cool and clear state of calm. Whatever or whoever is front of me is more real. My work is pleasurable. My relaxation is more fulfilling. My attentiveness is awakened. My mindfulness blooms.

Mindfulness teacher Sylvia Boorstein first introduced me to the use of a pair of thick brass cymbals joined by a leather thong, which I can carry in a pocket. They're called *tingsha*. Other people I know keep a small bowl bell in their backpack or purse. There are also apps that can play meditation bells for us at designated intervals. This is particularly apt when at a computer. Without an occasional reminder, I can lose all sense of time, and become disconnected from my environment.

Another form of the mindfulness bell is the Red Dot Practice. To prepare, buy some small, red, circular stickers from an office supply store. Then place a red dot at various strategic spots in your home or workplace — on the inside of a door, by a desk, or on a wall. Whenever you look at one of your red dots, consider it as a tiny stop sign. Pause, and enjoy a few conscious breaths. Mind the gap between breaths. Smile to contact your still point. Simply be.

Ultimately, you don't need a literal bell. Bells are everything and everyone we connect with! So we are always spontaneously reminded to be mindful all the time, if we heed the call. It could be the sound of a bird . . . a truck . . . or the wind through the trees. Even an unpleasant sound. It might be the sight of a cloud drifting, or a baby smiling . . . the fragrance of flowers, or warm sunlight on our bare skin. The stirring of a new feeling, or the recognition that our mind is hatching a plot. Simply stopping to breathe, consciously, three times, and coming home to our bodies in the present moment, is, itself, a mindfulness bell.

Mindfulness bell practice can hold delicious surprises. Once, I was teaching qigong (pronounced "chee goong") on the beach at Aquatic Park in San Francisco, and — *ding ding!* I heard a bicycle bell. Well, I couldn't stop. I was responsible to a class closely following my moves. So I dropped whatever images I'd had about teaching, or qigong, and more fully merged with my movement in that moment. I still recall the flowing freshness of the ocean breeze.

One time, halfway through a five-day retreat, after lunch, I entered the big hall, found my cushion, and sat down on the floor among my friends. At the sound of the bell, I joined my palms, made a half-bow, and enjoyed my breathing, waiting for the inevitable announcement of that day's unfolding events. I was flexible for a possible change of plans. Maybe our speaker was late, that sometimes happens. A few moments went by and still nobody said a thing. I looked across the aisle and saw my friend Chinh, looking at nothing in particular, with a gaze that said to me, "Ho hum, what's next, let's see." So I figured I was joining everyone in waiting to find out what would be next.

It wasn't until twenty breaths later that I realized there is no next. This is it. We're all just sitting here. And here I am, not "practicing" anything at all — just sitting and continuing to do so for thirty or forty minutes with nothing to gain, nothing to attain. No Zen to find in the Zen center except what I brought there. I felt tranquil, attentive, grateful just being still, and quietly happy to be so. Such a level of meditation is without need of "meditation."

It's good to be reminded to practice *non*practice. Letting be. When I'm sitting in formal meditation at home, I sometimes hear a church bell. I'm already doing nothing. So I let go of any idea of meditating, to be more vulnerable, fully aware of what's alive in the inexhaustible present moment while also growing more aware of awareness itself. As empty as a bell.

And when I'm arriving at my front porch — *ding ding ding!* — I often hear a passing cable car bell. Then I find myself coming home to coming home. As the Jamaican poet Derek Walcott says, "Greet yourself arriving at your own door."

When I first began my mindfulness-bell practice, I remember falling in love with the sound of the bell. I wanted to embrace its deep sound and hug it to my heart. Later, I came to appreciate the bell as echoing my own human condition. A bell has a physical body, yet with an intangible resonance extending beyond. As such, I've come to consider the mindfulness bell my good friend. Sometimes, I can't help but smile in grateful appreciation at how the ringing of a meditation bell can last for a full three breaths — a neat, adequate measure for emptying out, connecting, and beginning anew. Over the years, I've come to enjoy mindfulness bells as both a discipline and a release. As such, this epitomizes how the practice of awakening mindfulness is for me both commitment and surrender.

Or, in a word: *ding!*

a moral perspective

A moral perspective is not the dessert course, added to the end of the meal and optional. We can't be too rich or too poor to have one; it is the very core of how we live, how we get along with others, feel empathy for the plights of our fellow travelers, and try to shape our own lives and that of our children, loved ones, friends, and communities.

MAXINE CHERNOFF

Life is here and now. The past is history. The future is still a mystery. But today is a gift — that's why they call it the present. And yet, dwelling in the here and now may not always be enough. An Irish setter and a jewel thief are really great at being in the here and now. For a jewel thief, alertness is very much part of the job description. It comes with the terrain of a criminal lifestyle. And let's consider my neighbor Dave's big, red Irish setter, who he's been walking in Washington Square Park every afternoon since the dawn of time. One fine afternoon, after chatting with a friend, he looked around and saw his dear hound, true to the unwritten code of a happy animal lifestyle, trotting away with a total stranger, perfectly delighted to follow whomever showered him with attention and affection.

What's lacking for an Irish setter and a jewel thief is moral responsibility.

Relationality.

Spiritual teacher Rev. angel Kyodo williams tells us that if we were to just add the words *and others* to our attention to self, it would dramatically alter perception and outcome. This wise worldview awakens us to ourselves and the world at the same time. Taking responsibility for our intentions *and* their impact — along with regaining the power to choose our responses, instead of reacting from impulse — opens our space of growth and freedom.

Being a good person — leading a life styled around core values, nourishing what's wholesome and avoiding what's harmful — can be one of the most valuable gifts we can offer ourselves and others. We can nurture this gift through meditation: being aware of our inner experience and our outer experience, and also the relationships between the two. This is an important part of meditation; still, such meditation alone is not enough.

A fulfilling life that includes moral responsibility takes training, the way an athlete trains. To become a better swimmer, you'd look at your stroke, kick, and breathing, but also your diet and sleep habits, stamina, and ability to concentrate — in a word, your *lifestyle*. And it's a practice, the way a musician, no matter how famous, practices basics like scales, over and over. A moral lifestyle doesn't just fall from the sky on a shimmering silver platter, wrapped up neatly in elegant gift paper, and bound by a shiny red ribbon tied off in a fancy bow. It takes compassionate aspiration and powerful motivation, good guidelines and wholesome habits, as well as checking in on ourselves to see how we're doing. It requires, in a word, *intentionality.*

what is intentionality?

I went to the woods because I wished to live deliberately.
HENRY DAVID THOREAU

At birth, you're given a one-way ticket to this thing called "life." Don't waste it. Don't fall asleep. Make your conduct conscious. Intentional. Intention gives direction to our action, like threading a needle before sewing, or giving thanks before enjoying a meal. Have you ever encountered people lacking direction in life? They may appear solid in 3D, but seem "lost in space" somehow. They might also be adrift in terms of the fourth dimension, or their orientation in time. They're like a cork bobbing on the surface of the water hither and thither, following every little shift in the currents. In extreme cases, the "lost ones" are like sticks drowning in the ocean's depths, no longer knowing which way is up.

Intentionality points us where we need to go. Other species innately understand direction, literally. Almost half of all birds migrate annually, some even flying thousands of miles nonstop, without GPS. Our need for a sense of direction goes beyond points on a compass.

Knowing our internal true north helps us find and follow the path, in any situation. Our clear intentions remind us where we're coming from, so we can always position ourselves to go or grow to where we want to be in our journey. A lifestyle based on intention gives life purpose. This isn't necessarily a matter of rules to obey for reaching any fixed destination. Rather, it's about creatively connecting with our heart.

Over the centuries, we've been learning how to converse with each other about our meaning and purpose. In 1853, an abolitionist Unitarian minister named Theodore Parker expressed the idea that the arc of the moral universe is long, but it bends toward justice. Intentionality can incline us along that vector and help us bend its arc. It's a way of looking clearly at how and why we think and speak and do as we do. It orients us in relation to the deep goodness within and all around us — our true north, our true worth.

Deep down, we know right from wrong. Doing good makes us happy. And a common aspiration of all beings is simply that: to be happy. We are each capable of touching the unconditional love that's alive and quivering in every atom of ourselves and our world. So we might learn well how to understand, embody, and share that one love.

This doesn't imply being insanely driven by purpose like a runaway train. We just keep our feet on the trail, our eyes on the prize, and amble along. In the course of everyday living, we can always check to see if our aim is true. We often learn more from our human failings and foibles than we do from being always on target. If a storm shakes our branches, we return to our mindful breathing and take refuge in our roots extending deep in the soil of our true goodness.

When it comes time to act, we're not obsessively attached to the outcome. For instance, Zen master Kobun Chino Otogawa (Steve Jobs' former Zen teacher) was asked to teach Zen archery at Big Sur. For his first shot, he pulled back the bow, let it go, and watched his arrow go zinging over the target set up on a cliff and plunge down into the Pacific Ocean. Triumphantly, he shouted: "Bull's-eye!"

mindfulness blessings
gathas

Mindfulness bells teach us the discipline of pausing to return to the present moment. Yet without heart intention, being in the here and now may not be enough. A very simple example of life without intention is walking into a room, then forgetting why we came there. What we were going to do is a matter of intention. So we can intend to be mindful, not absentminded. We can always pause, to be conscious *and* intentional, connecting throughout the day.

Mindfulness needn't be an intermittent part of your life, like a faucet that turns off and on. It can be inherent in every moment. For instance, when I hold a glass of water, I know I'm holding a miracle. (That's why I hold it in both hands.) Even before I drink, I awaken my attention to how cherishable water is. Then, drinking, I can be as grateful as an infant at the bosom of life. A glass of H_2O may or may not contain holy water; it's my practice that makes it so. This I call a "blessing."

Here's another entry from the annals of absentmindedness. Have you ever sat down to eat a meal and then, a little later, found yourself facing an empty bowl and wondered, "Where did the food go?!" Without pausing to give thanks for the food, any meal can be like that. A mindfulness blessing is exactly that kind of pause — for a dedication or expression of appreciation or a pledge or a vow, concerning whatever's before us, right now.

This kind of blessing can make each moment sacred, consecrating it. Like prayer, it doesn't require permission. It can take place in an instant, on the spot. This can be a religion* of just two: you and whatever's before you. When you bless a glass of water, the water's no longer a thing or an "it," but a manifestation of the whole

---

* What does the thirteenth-century word *religion* really mean, anyway? It's usually believed to be taken from *religare*, which means "to bind together," as in obligation to monastic vows. This is also similar to *yoga* — "yoking" the physical and the spiritual — and also connecting with other people. Another reading takes it to mean "recollection," which is the original meaning of the Sanskrit word for mindfulness — *smriti* — calling something to mind, remembering to be present, to be attentive. Another possible origin, *religiens*, "careful," is the opposite of negligence *negligens*.

cosmos, a "thou." The glass of water I see on my table is part of my mind. And so, likewise, my mind is in the glass of water. Thus a mindfulness blessing needn't assume that anything is over and above our own mind, nor any less divine.

These devotional verses furnish beautiful, caring lenses for focusing intention in everyday life. They're compact reminders that mindfulness is always applicable, even to all the nooks and crannies of daily life. It takes a bit of practice at first for these little personal rituals to become second nature. Meanwhile, we might observe how they can imbue our circumstances and activities with fuller concentration and deeper meaning.

Dwelling in mindfulness, every moment is an opportunity to live deeply. For instance, let's say I am still holding a glass of water. I can pause to bring to mind how far it's traveled (275 miles, in my case, from Mt. Shasta via Tuolumne Meadows). And so precious! There's a saying in Lakota, *mni wiconi*, which means "water is life," "water is alive." As a daily reminder, over my kitchen sink sits this mindfulness blessing from Thich Nhat Hanh:

> Water comes from high mountain sources.
> Water runs deep in the Earth.
> Miraculously, water comes to us and sustains all life.
> My gratitude is filled to the brim.

When I bring to mind the preciousness of water, intention's baked into my initial impulse to drink. It was there in my inclination toward action even before I reached for the faucet. When the water arrives within my grasp, I'm careful not to waste a drop, mindful of its myriad manifestations along its immense journey to my kitchen . . . as river, as ocean, as cloud, as snow . . . and mindful of the many hands that helped bring it to me. As with water, so too with earth, air, and fire. Our universe is mostly some very ordinary elements. Just as it is. And everything is absolutely sacred. Just as it is.

A booklet of mindful meditation verses, compiled by Chinese meditation master Duti, was given to Thich Nhat Hanh as a novice entering Tu Hieu Monastery in Hue. There, these short verses are known by the Sanskrit word *gatha* (pronounced "gotta"). The first gatha he was given for study begins: "Waking up this morning I smile . . ."

I've illuminated my copy with colored pencils and pinned it to my windowsill. Yet this is more than a nice thought or pretty imagery. We can make it a *practice*, saying the first line to ourselves with our in-breath, then the second line with our out-breath. This way, our intention engages and unites our mind-body-spirit as one. A little later, we move on to practice the next pair of parallel lines (couplet), the same way.

This one verse can be used for casual contemplation, or it can serve as a blueprint for a twenty- to forty-minute meditation, to start the day in harmony.

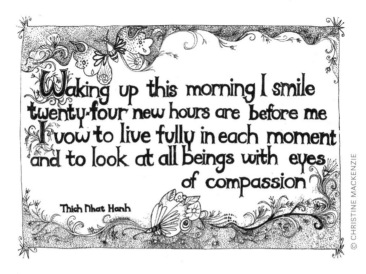

Waking up this morning I smile
twenty-four new hours are before me
I vow to live fully in each moment
and to look at all beings with eyes
of compassion

Thich Nhat Hanh

© CHRISTINE MACKENZIE

Neuroscientists find that our mind-body establishes a baseline for our experience, like a thermostat on a heater. By practicing this mindfulness blessing first thing in the morning, I'm raising the bar for my physical comfort zone, my emotional set point, my mind's natural resting state, my psychic horizon, and my kindness quotient — a good benchmark for the day ahead.

Moreover, there's also what feels to me like a magic trick to practicing this: going from being awake, to awakening. Just because my eyes are open doesn't mean I'm awake. Actually saying the words *waking up* asks me to pause, recognize that I'm awake, and make awakening a conscious activity. Beginning my day this way, I genuinely awaken as I awaken. Until I do, I'm like a bystander to my life. Smiling can be like sitting in the driver's seat. Scientists have found that smiling sends a chemical message from our mouth muscles to our nervous system, saying, "It's okay to dial down those fight-flight-or-freeze responses. I'm safe, and taking care." We're being compassionate for our human default mode of vestigial, reactive habits, which tries to play backseat driver. Our eyes of compassion can help heal and transform this chronic reactivity into conscious response.

Awakening can occur at any moment, not just after a night's sleep. Throughout my day, I pause to breathe and remember how good it is to awaken, to be fully engaged with whatever's in front of my nose. Over time, I'm building up a "muscle memory" for this, just like riding a bicycle, driving, swimming, or dancing, which I've come to know by heart.

Thich Nhat Hanh has introduced this practice to the West through a book of several dozen verses of mindfulness blessings for adults and kids. It's titled *Present Moment Wonderful Moment*. After you get the hang of it, by all means, make up some of your own. For example, mindfulness teacher Kenley Neufeld has a short recipe for a kind of psychic protection to see us through difficult times:

> Is there something you're struggling with or that you would like to transform in your life? Try writing four short lines you can memorize, to recite when the issue arises. For example:

I see the car in front of me.
I don't need to hurry.
Arriving in the present moment
I water the seed of patience in me (and smile).

Awareness of *breath* is a grounding in mindful contemplation; awareness of *intention* is a touchstone of mindful conduct. Together, they sharpen our attention and arouse our care, molding a mindful lifestyle where healing compassion and transformative wisdom can arise and flourish, for ourselves and others. This is a blessing, indeed.

the power of pausing

There's a word in the Spanish language that we don't really have an equivalent for in English. The word is *pausadamente*. It beautifully expresses a quality of taking your time, preceding with reflectiveness, deliberateness, with a kind of dignity . . . being pauseful when we act and speak.

CHARLES F. HERR

Humans are hardwired for stories. Stories provide a lens for us to gaze through, to awaken our imagination and teach us by example. So here are a couple of life sketches about the power of pausing, being pauseful, starting off with a true tale of my own.

ALONE, WITH OTHERS

I was sitting on a morning bus heading downtown. My nose was in a book, something spiritual I'd kept in my pocket for the journey. We were passing through a populous neighborhood, stopping at every block and taking on passengers, and we were soon all packed together like sardines in a can. Ordinarily, I'm fine with being in thick crowds, having gotten used to a slower, more collective rhythm and flow of humanity on buses. Well, this morning, contemplating an especially lofty passage in my little book, I'd failed to notice that we'd already gone through the tunnel. That meant my stop would be up next. *Uh-oh!* Normally, I'd already be in line to get off. Now, still holding in my mind the profound words I'd just been reading, I tried to hurry ahead.

I stood up without so much as a pause, and, squeezing myself over the knees of the person sitting next to me, stepped into the crammed aisle, where people who were ready to get off stood mixed in with people who were staying on. I picked my way past two of the five or six people not getting off when, suddenly someone shouted, "OuuuwCH!" Loudly. At me!

(*Whoops!*)

Looking around, I discovered I'd stepped on someone's toes. Bare toes. In sandals. *Dang!* I was so busy looking ahead, trying to get out, I'd forgotten to look down, where I stepped. I stopped and stuttered my apologies. But . . . no! The Chinese gentleman, a little younger than me, whose toes I'd ungallantly stomped, looked me over head to toe, in one, swift, up-and-down glance — taking in the screwy expression on my face, my little spiritual book in hand, my own sandals — and came back at me with, "Oh, I bet you're *real sorry*, aren't you!? Like *hell*!" Crestfallen, I felt a river of bitter guilt engulf me. Those timeless truths in which I'd been immersed were now mere ink on paper — noble sentiments smashed like a sandcastle beneath a thirty-foot wave. *Blam!*

Anyhow, it had happened. I could see nothing left to be done, as the bus had come to its stop, and the man moved to the back to sit down, while I went the other way, ahead, and out. Demolished.

WHAT'S THE CAPTION TO THIS PICTURE?

Caption: *Be here now.*

Yes — but . . . also . . .

. . . awakening means being mindful of wisdom *in action*, as well as in being. A pause can provide that space where an impulsive *reaction* can be changed into an intentional *response*. A better caption then might be, *Pausing First Can Be More Productive Than Acting*. I forgot to pause; I'd missed that precious beat for self-awareness.

My failure on the bus also spotlights how we seem to harbor a shadow side to our nature. Like the wind, we never quite see it, only its effects. If we miss the mark often enough, we might discover a pattern. It can feel like an inner gremlin is lurking within our personality. (I call mine "Murgatroyd.") This puts a face on our invisible collective karma as humans, still reacting with survival instincts that have been ingrained in us since our times as hunter-gatherers in ancient jungles, but not as suitable for contemporary daily living. However we picture it, we know from experience our shadow side can nip at our ankles and trip us up unless we recognize, accept, and deal with it appropriately.

Caption: *Look both ways.*

My bumbling blunder also highlights a danger zone in mindful lifestyle known as *spiritual bypassing*. Here, spirituality distances us from what really matters. I was hiding behind my spiritual practice, avoiding being present to everyday reality, where true spirit dwells — in this case, on a crowded public bus. The Zen way would be to ride a bus to ride a bus rather than ride a bus in order to read a book. (It would be doubly ironic if the book had been titled *Our Shadow Side*.) In this case, perhaps a better caption would be *If You're Going to Talk the Talk, You've Got to Walk the Walk*.

But that's not all. My big boo-boo reflects the universal human tendency to seek pleasure (a book) and avoid what's difficult (a crowded bus). We can spend our entire lives bouncing between these two poles. Running after and running away (plus running and hiding).

Life is brief. Recognizing that, we can vow to take care of ourselves and others while we can. This is precisely the point of skillful intention: recognizing needless suffering, understanding it, and healing and transforming it.

Caption: *Stop running: breathe, smile, and keep caring.*

I'd like to share two more vignettes underscoring the relevance of our pausing to be intentional and relational. I hope they deepen your appreciation of the power of your own, internal pause button. They might give you insight into others' buttons too, the same as yours.

DEATH ROW

Is it enough for us to be aware of life's moral virtues and vices, without our understanding them through our personal practice? Here's a slice of life that might dramatize that question a bit more vividly. Clinton Duffy grew up in a prison town. He came to work in the penal system there. For eleven years, he served as warden of San Quentin. During his term as warden, he got to know a deputy sheriff from Los Angeles. This deputy would bring prisoners to him every week or so, sometimes as many as one or two hundred at a time. After he'd delivered his shipment, he'd stay in Warden Duffy's office to chat. They'd talk about sports, politics, the weather, and, sooner or later, the death penalty. The deputy was an advocate for the death penalty, whereas the warden wasn't so sure.

Well, one day, the deputy sheriff murdered his spouse. Three days after being brought to Death Row, Clinton visited him in his cell. Finally, he had to ask, "How come you didn't think of the death penalty?" The deputy confessed, "Never at any time did I think of the death penalty, until after."

Later on, San Quentin built a gas chamber. They hired inmates to build it. One of these workers, a former thief, was later released after serving three years. Then, three years later, he was brought back, this time to Death Row. He'd killed some of his own relatives plus a friend who all tried to break up his romance with a half-sister. The warden asked him the same question and again was told the same thing, in a different way: "When the devil gets into you, you think of nothing else."

During his career, Clinton Duffy witnessed over one hundred and fifty executions, legally officiated at the execution of eighty-eight men and two women, and participated in sixty legal hangings. After retirement, he devoted the remainder of his life traveling across the country, lecturing for the abolishment of capital punishment.

If I may, I'd like to pause here for a few comments on what we've seen so far. Sooner or later (and sooner rather than later), we need to recognize and work with our inclination to harm ourselves and others. We aren't perfect. Difficult emotions can easily trigger us. Our unwholesome impulses need to be restrained and retrained.

To do so, we wrestle with another problem: living in the delusion that we don't harbor this harmful inclination. But turning away is so easy. We deny that our vision has a blind spot and try to cover our tracks. Thai mindfulness master Ajahn Chah likens the mind's tendency toward self-justification to a criminal who rationalizes his misbehavior by thinking he can always hire a good lawyer who'll solve everything.

I'm hesitant to use the word *sin* here. Such a small word, yet it can mark what's arguably Western civilization's primary myth, not to mention heavy personal baggage, hurtful memories, and even deep trauma. Yet in Hebrew, the word *sin* can just mean "missing the mark."* We all make mistakes. It softens my heart to realize how everyone is challenged by missing the mark. However they deal with it, they're all just like me. This recognition of common humanity awakens my compassion, for myself and others.

Our shortcomings define our humanity. Aware of our tendency to err, understanding our vulnerability can reveal our fundamental goodness. Then our intention can be aimed toward that goodness.

THE HUMAN CONDITION

Our study of shortcomings needn't be morbid, it just needs to be honest and practical. Recognizing and understanding how deeply fallibility runs in us can prompt a cultivation of compassion. This doesn't switch our foibles off, but it does soften them and add spaciousness around them. Over time, compassion lets us see beyond our flaws and lets love awaken. It invites us to care, easing our suffering and that of others. In that light, I'd like to share with you just one more brief tale about the human condition.

I was the guest of a Japanese Pure Land temple in Venice Beach, California, offering an evening talk to the

---

*I've witnessed a Zen archer hit the bull's-eye with their first shot, then split that arrow with their second shot. Still, archery is only an analogy. You know the *feeling* when you're on target, when your conscience is clear . . . and when you've missed the mark.

temple youth group, then an afternoon haiku workshop. Just after I arrived, I stood outside the back door with the temple's young priest, Rev. John Iwohara. Enjoying the early evening dusk together, I could sense from his very presence he had a depth and inclusivity of care.

Well, we fell into a conversation. One thing led to another, and, without fanfare and speaking from his heart, he confessed to me that his deepest meditation was this: he knew that if he were to somehow find himself trapped with many other people in a huge vat of oil, and someone outside the vat was turning up the flames beneath and the oil started to boil, his first impulse would be to climb over the others — even his own son if he had to — and push them down to get out. He paused as a gentle breeze passed by, and then he added that this was what his practice addressed every day.

In the dwindling light, I nodded in silence. I knew this was only a *thought*, but thoughts influence words, which influence actions, which influence further thoughts. The whole process can collectively be called "karma." Fortunately, nothing is permanent. While our karma weaves patterns in our lives, we can always change — beginning with intention, which underlies karma. So his compassionate thought gave me pause, indeed.

In his Pure Land Buddhist tradition, when we awaken to the fact that we're all, at bottom, utterly foolish, inescapably acting out of plain ignorance and self-centered desires, only then do we viably opt to arouse compassion as our aspiration. Only then can we honestly approach the redemptive power of compassion. Since we're capable of compassion for ourselves, think how much more compassion must be there for a murderer. Our lives may seem, necessarily, limited, viewed in historical time; dwelling in compassion, we experience a state that's boundless. Immeasurable.

I hope these three stories illuminate the path of intention for you. I'd like to invite you now to journey further along on it, framing intention within a moral perspective. As we do so, we might ask what underlies our intentions. Pausing to explore this theme, we can then cap our tour with practical guidelines for training our ethical impulses in daily life.

motivation, the game changer

We see what happens when we remain unconscious, reacting from our unevolved nature, functioning on autopilot rather than responding intentionally. And even when our conduct is conscious, we need to take responsibility if our intent has an undesired impact. Now I'd like to raise the stakes. Adding inmost inspiration to intention can stimulate our motivation. Such a heart motivation can then be a model for guiding all our initial impulses.

Someone once asked the Dalai Lama what he did first in the morning. Flashing his ever-present smile, he answered, "Shape motivation!" Intention guides action; motivation is what underlies intention. In a very fundamental way, it's where we're coming from. So it's good to take a step back from time to time and ask, "What's my motivation for mindful awakening?"

Behind and beneath any laundry list of wished-for benefits, what's your inmost aspiration? What's the touchstone that underlies your initial intention, every time? Let's say you want to be of service but wish to first get clear within yourself: totally awaken first, then help others awaken. I utterly respect that. Yet, personally, I think this might work if you lived in an isolated cabin in the woods. Me, I'm a city dweller, continually negotiating human interchange as part of the everyday landscape.

To reframe the question, what happens when you consider awakening together? For instance, taking another cue from the Dalai Lama, I might decide to engage mindfulness not only for myself but also for and with others — out of "selfish altruism." That is, I want everyone to be safe and secure, at peace, happy, and thriving, partly because I honestly don't like being in a world where people live close to the edge of losing it and going under, big time.

So consider how it would feel if your initial motivation for mindfulness were for the good of others, for the good of all creation even, of which you happen to be an important part. Such is my vow. There's no ulterior motive. Sincerely wanting to awaken, I know I can use all the help I can get. Having all of creation on my side lends me powerful momentum and support. Plus, it's a win-win decision. Our personal inner tangle and the world's outer tangle are intertangled. To untangle one is to simultaneously disentangle the other. And acting on behalf of all beings is critical training in a selfless, nondual worldview.

However you frame it, motivation is a simple lever that can move your world.

the golden rule

We're ethically motivated when our intentions are based on conscious values. But where do our values come from? Often we learn our values through role models, our family, our ancestry, and society. I can also explore values in daily interactions, such as when someone asks me questions about myself. I listen deeply, as what people choose to ask reflects what they value.

Actually, many sets of ethical guidelines might all be boiled down to one: the Golden Rule. From Christianity to Islam, from Baha'i to Zoroastrianism, and from indigenous spirituality to humanist existentialism, this is like a golden thread running through civilizations, like a single figure in a complex carpet interwoven by the diverse cultures on our blue planet.

The Golden Rule is a tenet that advises us to treat others as we would want them to treat us. Its nondual wisdom of seeing others as not different from ourselves clears our view. And it's an agreement: we are all in this together. This reintroduces us to our relationality. Our personal experiences of it will vary, of course. For instance, anyone routinely mistreated could have more experiential insight into it than me. Yet the value of the Golden Rule doesn't vary. It's one truth, with multiple applications. Its value becomes bankable when we realize that it begins with us. Setting intention from such an active, awakened perspective surely results in our becoming better people. To identify with other beings as closely as you do yourself . . . world peace, as simple as that.

mindfulness trainings

With vigorous motivation as a base and the Golden Rule as our pole star, we look for training. How can we clarify and apply our intentions in daily life? Fortunately, we inherit classic precedents. For example, all three Abrahamic religions teach ten primary precepts.* We might boil these down into five themes:

---

* The Hebrew for the "Ten Commandments" is *Aseret HaDibbrot* — the ten sayings, utterances, or statements. The word *dibbrot* itself bears no connotation of punishment or reward. You could say it's the way the Beloved has of showing us the way things are (so follow the Way).

1 Reverence for life
2 Generosity
3 Love
4 Communication
5 Sobriety

Some mindfulness practitioners review these every morning, perhaps from a sheet of paper by the bathroom mirror that might read something like this:

On behalf of myself and all beings,
I intend to refrain from consciously hurting anyone.
I intend to refrain from overtly or covertly taking what is not mine.
I intend to abstain from sexuality that is exploitive or abusive.
I intend to be sure that my speech is kind as well as true.
I intend to refrain from addictive behaviors that confuse my mind and lead to heedlessness.

Such mindfulness trainings outline a gold standard against which we can measure truth, and our responsibility to it, for regular review. I'd like to share a version as envisioned and revisioned over the years by Thich Nhat Hanh and the Plum Village community. They're invaluable for studying, observing, and realizing our aspirations to become warm, trustworthy, authentic human beings, for ourselves and others. I consider them as my universal survival kit. As you'll see, they're quite contemporary. They serve as sturdy, dynamic, daily points of departure for awakening mindfulness. My weekly circle reads and discusses them every full moon. Thousands of mindfulness practitioners engage them regularly. Please offer them your serene mind, your open heart, and a reflective ear, open to what resonates within.

THE FIRST MINDFULNESS TRAINING
Reverence for Life

Aware of the suffering caused by the destruction of life, I am committed to cultivating the insight of interbeing and compassion and learning ways to protect the lives of people, animals, plants, and minerals. I am determined not to kill, not to let others kill, and not to support any act of killing in the world, in my thinking, or in my way of life. Seeing that harmful actions arise from anger, fear, greed, and intolerance, which in turn come from dualistic and discriminative thinking, I will cultivate openness, nondiscrimination, and nonattachment to views in order to transform violence, fanaticism, and dogmatism in myself and in the world.

THE SECOND MINDFULNESS TRAINING
True Happiness

Aware of the suffering caused by exploitation, social injustice, stealing, and oppression, I am committed to practicing generosity in my thinking, speaking, and acting. I am determined not to steal and not to possess anything that should belong to others, and I will share my time, energy, and material resources with those who are in need. I will practice looking deeply to see that the happiness and suffering of others are not separate from my own happiness and suffering; that true happiness is not possible without understanding and compassion; and that running after wealth, fame, power, and sensual pleasures can bring much suffering and despair. I am aware that happiness depends on my mental attitude and not on external conditions, and that I can live happily in the present moment simply by remembering that I already have more than enough conditions to be happy. I am committed to practicing Right Livelihood so that I can help reduce the suffering of living beings on Earth and reverse the process of global warming.

THE THIRD MINDFULNESS TRAINING
True Love

Aware of the suffering caused by sexual misconduct, I am committed to cultivating responsibility and learning ways to protect the safety and integrity of individuals, couples, families, and society. Knowing that sexual desire is not love, and that sexual activity motivated by craving always harms myself as well as others, I am determined not to engage in sexual relations without true love and a deep, long-term commitment made known to my family and friends. I will do everything in my power to protect children from sexual abuse and to prevent couples and families from being broken by sexual misconduct. Seeing that body and mind are one, I am committed to learning appropriate ways to take care of my sexual energy and cultivating lovingkindness, compassion, joy, and inclusiveness — which are the four basic elements of true love — for my greater happiness and the greater happiness of others. Practicing true love, we know that we will continue beautifully into the future.

THE FOURTH MINDFULNESS TRAINING
Loving Speech and Deep Listening

Aware of the suffering caused by unmindful speech and the inability to listen to others, I am committed to cultivating loving speech and compassionate listening in order to relieve suffering and to promote reconciliation and peace in myself and among other people, ethnic and religious groups, and nations. Knowing that words can create happiness or suffering, I am committed to speaking truthfully using words that inspire confidence, joy, and hope. When anger is manifesting in me, I am determined not to speak. I will practice mindful breathing and walking in order to recognize and to look deeply into my anger. I know that the roots of anger can be found in my wrong perceptions and lack of understanding of the suffering in myself and in the other person. I will speak and listen in a way that can help myself and the other person to transform suffering and see the way out of difficult situations. I am determined not to spread news that I do not know to be certain and not to utter words that can cause division or discord. I will practice Right Diligence to nourish my capacity for understanding, love, joy, and inclusiveness and gradually transform the anger, violence, and fear that lie deep in my consciousness.

THE FIFTH MINDFULNESS TRAINING
Nourishment and Healing

Aware of the suffering caused by unmindful consumption, I am committed to cultivating good health, both physical and mental, for myself, my family, and my society by practicing mindful eating, drinking, and consuming. I will practice looking deeply into how I consume the Four Kinds of Nutriments, namely edible foods, sense impressions, volition, and consciousness. I am determined not to gamble, or to use alcohol, drugs, or any other products that contain toxins, such as certain websites, electronic games, TV programs, films, magazines, books, and conversations. I will practice coming back to the present moment to be in touch with the refreshing, healing, and nourishing elements in me and around me, not letting regrets and sorrow drag me back into the past nor letting anxieties, fear, or craving pull me out of the present moment. I am determined not to try to cover up loneliness, anxiety, or other suffering by losing myself in consumption. I will contemplate interbeing and consume in a way that preserves peace, joy, and well-being in my body and consciousness, and in the collective body and consciousness of my family, my society, and the Earth.

TRAININGS FOR A CREATIVE, FULFILLING, BENEFICIAL LIFESTYLE

Mindfulness trainings are voluntary, pragmatic, and relational. They resonate harmoniously with equivalents found in a range of spiritual traditions. Yet they're bottom-up, rather than top-down. Lived experience rather than dogma or decree is their standard. They're not motivated by punishment or reward but by self-improvement.

Each training is titled with a primary virtue, an aspiration for the best within each of us. Then each begins in recognizing how suffering is always present from the get-go, implicitly, to be understood and transformed. Each also points us toward what's beneficial and steers us away from what's harmful. In reality, wholesome and unwholesome are marbled together. So there's healthy wisdom in maintaining a nondual perspective that sees how one implies the other, as two sides of the same coin.

Of course, situations are not always clear-cut. We may not always know what to do. Still, we have models to draw upon. We can apply our natural goodness as recognized in previous situations to current similar situations *by extension*. What's useful in a traffic jam (patience, for instance) may also apply at an office meeting. This process implies ethics can be a lifestyle of continual creative discovery.

THE PROOF OF THE PUDDING IS IN THE EATING

Mindfulness trainings can help us steer clear of holding on to theoretical wisdom without putting it into action. Otherwise, we might only be reinforcing our faith in our mental fabrications, our mind always trying to think our way out of any uncomfortable situation. But when insight into the way things are spontaneously arises, compassion arises at the same time. And compassion without action isn't very meaningful. As Thich Nhat Hanh reminds us, "Compassion is a verb."

Neuroscientist Paul Bach-y-Rita devised an experiment that illustrates the interaction of perception and action, or how perception *is* action. He connected a blind person to a camera that translated its images into tactile sensations. If the blind person stayed motionless, they felt no stimulation. But the more the person moved, the more they would be able to experience objects in 3D, judge how to navigate amongst the objects, and direct the camera's gaze. So too can we direct our mindfulness, our compassion, our love, our cleaving to truth, toward ourselves and our world — through action.

CULTIVATING GOODNESS ISN'T HEAVY LIFTING

If we're archers, we could use training on how to pay sharper attention, balance our stance, refine our aim, pull back the bow farther, let go more completely, and take responsibility for the outcome. Zen archers know they're already perfect yet recognize they can use a little improvement. This is a great way to approach mindfulness trainings too.

Viewing life with nondual wisdom, we can be innovative and intertwine cause and effect (typically considered two separate things). We usually think of joy as preceding a smile, but sometimes a smile can precede the joy. Similarly, in Zen, we assume a posture of awakened, quiet dignity *before* meditation. Why? Because we don't need to seek awakening; we are *already* awakened. We just need the opportunity to reconnect with our true nature and grow more intimate with it.

Ethical trainings can furnish us with a model of how we might likely behave when our inherent compassionate wisdom manifests in us.

We need only recognize that our essential nature is already virtuous, yet prone to error, then practice from there. Actually, I saw this confirmed for me just the other morning, while I was standing on a corner, waiting for the light to change. Across the street, an older man going from the drugstore to the parking lot suddenly fell over backward into the street. Immediately, two passersby stopped and went over to him. Then two more arrived, and soon all four were helping him up, then staying to make sure he was alright. The scene provided a clear mirror of an essential truth in life: we don't have to manufacture compassion; we uncover it through action. Mindfulness trainings provide us with a similar mirror.

LOOK AROUND

Mindfulness isn't necessarily about awakening within our interior life only. Otherwise it might be considered merely navel-gazing. Awakening wisdom teaches me how my exterior and interior life are not separate. What happens in the world is happening within me, and vice versa. A committed, *engaged* practice of mindfulness invites me to observe and work with the imbalances implicit in social relations. Social conditions often require proper study for skillful observation and practice to take place. Independent scholar Ed Ng has deftly articulated some of these conditions as "personal exposure to vulnerability, uneven material conditions, power relations, and my position in all of it." Mindfulness practice provides a safe space of refuge in which I can awaken, and stay woke, to such themes in my lived world.

And mindfulness shows me how hope need not be just an emotion or belief, but a conscious course of action, for confirmation. Without such hope, I don't know how I would survive.

A PATH WITH A HEART

Awakening mindfulness takes courage. And in the root of the word *courage* we can hear the French word for heart: *coeur*. So mindfulness trainings encourage us to listen fearlessly to our heart. In setting intention, I ground myself in my breathing to be in touch with my body's heart, where I feel my intentions usually connect from; my actions tend to connect from my physical center, below my navel. Awareness of vital body centers leads me away from the concept that everything's happening in my cranium.

Sincere and truthful, heartful and wise, mindfulness trainings open us to healing and transformation, for ourselves and our relations. For instance, the trainings encourage us to notice where we hurt. Too often we flinch and look away from our suffering or hide it under a bandage or medicate it or fill it up with stuff. Easy ways out. They're the status quo of a mass culture of entertainment, which discounts true virtue and preys instead on greed and fear, cynicism and despair. Yet it's our soft spots of vulnerability that reveal to us our heart, our core capacity for true goodness. If we don't resist confronting our hurts but recognize and even contend with them, here's where we "build our humanity and keep it alive," as author Maxine Hong Kingston puts it.

If these trainings don't provoke questions, listen deeper. For instance, what does "reverence for life" say about war? Abortion? Vegetarianism? Might "being made known to family and friends" compromise a gay relationship that doesn't want to be outed? Is a recreational drug alright if it doesn't contain toxins? And so on. Mindfulness trainings are to be wrestled with, tested through action, then viewed in the mirror of life's continual, creative feedback. This means to study, observe, and practice being human. No more, no less.

SPEAKING FROM PERSONAL EXPERIENCE

I can only speak from my own experience. Heart-to-heart, here are some of my personal insights. I'm still learning that when I miss the mark, I needn't beat myself up over it. I can let it go. I am learning how to try better next time. And when I'm feeling the stirring of an inner grizzly bear, I feel solid in knowing I can take refuge in my mindful breathing. I know I can wait until it's safe to proceed, without claw marks on my ankles, and later take stock of the bear's reappearance in my landscape.

Although I'm in my seventies as of this writing, I haven't banished my inner gremlins once and for all. Still, over the years they've been shrinking to a more manageable scale. Lately, I've revisualized my inner grizzly bear as an open-armed gray teddy bear. (*Grah!*) If I'm at the dinner table and recognize when one of the imps (anger, fear, envy, jealousy, and so on) begins to stir from the carpet and wants to crawl up onto my ankle, I can confront it with the same awareness that recognizes a breath, a perception, a feeling, or a thought at the inception of its arising. I can say, "Hello, Murgatroyd. I see you coming. Gee, I'm sorry, but I just can't donate my leg for your lunch today, you poor, poor dear — so deprived, so depraved. Thank you for reminding me I'm a still-evolving human being. Now please go back to where you came from. Back to the jungle, which I no longer inhabit." Not having to worry about getting mauled or having to do damage control all the time clears my path of obstruction, making room for other more beneficial traits to take root and blossom in my heart's garden.

When I mindfully observe formations of anger or fear arising in me, I trust my ability to take care of these toxic states, based on my having done so before. For example, as a boy, I aspired to be part of the "Angry Young Men" movement that was in the air. Eventually, I realized my highly cultivated animosity was an inefficient source of fuel and counterproductive. I discovered that if I gave in to my impulse to pick up a burning coal and throw it at someone, I'd be the only one burned. Holding on to anger, I learned, is like drinking poison and expecting the other person to die.

With practice, I looked deeply within and, over time, was able to understand the manifestations of my anger at their root, and I began to heal and transform their energy. And I began cultivating seeds of forgiveness, kindness, and generosity instead. As I continue to do so, I'm also using my successful work on anger as a model for working on my fear: fear of failure, FOMO (fear of missing out), fear of change, fear of pain, and the thermonuclear fear that gives birth to all the others, fear of death. Brave alternatives to fear are trust, kindness, and joy. I still feel anger and fear but, thanks to the wisdom of nonself, I less readily identify myself with them.

I've found that dealing skillfully with negative energies can liberate beautiful positive energies, just waiting to slide me into a future my heart's wanted to inhabit all along. When, for instance, I look deeply at the mindfulness training of right speech, I might pay attention to how often my speech is disparaging, even violent — for instance, "being on *deadline*" or "making a *killing*." Monitoring my vocabulary and shedding negative words and phrases, I discover how much useful energy gets freed up. Since words shape thoughts and actions, I liberate my mind and deeds as well. And I am grateful for how pausing generates a space where I can check my intent and also take responsibility for its impact.

I've incorporated mindfulness trainings into my regular routine formally since 1996. I can attest to their being one of the most concrete ways I know of practicing mindfulness. I never fail to marvel at how closely integrated their guidelines are for the development of both my moral values and my consciousness, and how powerful this can be for overcoming suffering. I might add that Thich Nhat Hanh uses "trainings" as another word the Buddha used besides "precepts" to describe these practices.

But enough about my personal experience. I'd like to give the last word here on precepts, in general, to my dear contemporary Frank Ostaseski, who defines his own five precepts for service as "invitations." (That works too.) Cofounder of America's first Buddhist hospice, he's gone on to become a world-class teacher for all of us wanting to know what death can teach us about living fully. Leading retreats, he often begins with traditional precepts. He explains:

Mindfulness does not set us free . . . wisdom does. So it's helpful to have a basis for wisdom, and ethics can be such a support. Also the mindfulness develops our understanding of the precepts, and so there is this symbiotic exchange between precepts and mindfulness practice. Finally there is power in a vow, which is what the precepts are . . . a way of living by vow. They strengthen commitment, which gives rise to faith, which generates increased energy, which supports mindfulness, which deepens calmness, which allows for the cultivation of insight and developing wisdom.

study. observe. practice.

Studying and applying mindfulness trainings is an expression of my happiness at all I have yet to discover, about myself and the world. To integrate these trainings practically in your own life, here's a tried-and-true strategy that can equally apply to meditation and wisdom — and learning in general. I've learned this from a phrase common in Vietnamese Zen. In English it has the same initials as the familiar phrase "standard operating procedure" — S. O. P. (a step-by-step guide for carrying out any operation). Here, SOP stands for "Study. Observe. Practice."

We begin with *study*. This kind of study comes from teachings, heard or read. Things you feed your head or that come through your five senses. Either way, meaning is there, but is yet to be personally processed. For that, we need *observation*.

Observation implies contemplation . . . reflection . . . inquiry. Is what I'm studying true or false? Could it be beneficial or harmful? Measured against previous experience, how does it fit into my lived world? Do I observe this in others as well as myself?

Understanding others might seem like a luxury given how there's enough to yet understand about myself. Yet their stories are about me too. So wise observation of others can prompt self-realization. What I admire or despise or merely notice in others' behavior reflects what's already there within my own mind, otherwise I wouldn't recognize it.

Reflecting on our lives and observing life around us, we see where and how our studies might apply. We can verify our studies if they match up with our experience. The proof is in the *practice*. We always come back to practicality as our touchstone. Without putting what we learn into action, our observations and studies cannot catch a light or cast a shadow. We're only accumulating knowledge then, like someone who hoards stuff thinking it will serve a purpose "someday," until they finally need to shovel their way out in order to see daylight again.

SOP means we find out for ourselves, without taking anything for granted. We're studying with our own lives as textbooks. Reading the world thus, this is truly lifelong learning. Come on down to this university of the universe. Tuition's free. Classmates become best friends. The faculty is the finest in the land — our own awakened inner guides. Plus, there are bells of mindfulness on every campus, reminding us:

Now is the time.

This is it.

Study. Observation. Practice. All three are necessary for healthy development. Without a good object of study, we lack a solid basis for contemplation, or direction. Without critical reflection, our practice won't be as meaningful or deep or as fulfilling as it could be. And without practice we're only bystanders, viewing life through conceptual filters rather than living large according to our finest instincts.

Study. Observation. Practice. All three work together. Putting experience-molded insight into practice will, over time, generate seeds for further study, creating robust, positive feedback loops, spiraling like the DNA helix or the way a fern unfolds.

The key is in the practice. Practice sets up a matrix for further study and observation in one's own lived world and puts the three prompts in perpetual motion. In this way, anything and everything is a vehicle for awakening mindfulness through study, observation, and practice.

Study. Observe. Practice. Give thanks. Play. Thrive.

what does it mean to be human?
an evolutionary perspective

To cap our exploration of responsibility, let's take a couple steps back, for a panoramic perspective. (Please excuse the extremely broad brush.) Whenever we feel pushed or pulled by habitual cravings and aversions, they have roots in our ancestral, animal karma. It's good to note this. When we gain awareness of such situations and make a conscious choice to restrain or retrain our vestigial instincts, we're not only evolving as individuals, we're also tapping into a shift in our evolution as a species. In our six-million-year-old chronicles as Homo sapiens, a great shift occurred back in the Middle Stone Age, 70,000 years ago: self-awareness. This critical ability for monitoring our behavior and our inner landscape became the fulcrum for milestone changes in civilization. Yet self-awareness is still an evolving field. Psychologists, for instance, didn't begin studying self-awareness until the 1970s.

Keeping to a broad view, we see another awesome leap in consciousness occurring roughly between the eighth and third centuries BCE, relatively suddenly. How do we account for the Buddha, Confucius, the Hebrew prophets, Lao-Tzu, the pre-Socratic philosophers, Zoroaster, and other highly evolved, self-aware human beings popping up all around the planet in relatively the same window of time? And they're coming at a time when civilizations, themselves, are taking great leaps. Tribal and political boundaries are consolidating and expanding; coinage and markets are also appearing on the scene; reason and science are taking precedence over ritual; and people are turning away from punishment-reward systems and looking for guidelines for moral conscience (the Good), for themselves, their nation, and humanity.

It's often known as the Axial Age, *axial* meaning "turning." Historians now point to striking similarities between those times and ours, with its communications revolutions, globalization, economic transformations, disruptive technologies, and a more secularized society. Whether you call this a great turning, a paradigm shift, or a tipping point, you too might feel a change of consciousness in the air. Reflections of this can be seen, for example, in interdisciplinary collaborations between psychology, anatomy, evolution, philosophy, and physics, where mind-body studies are yielding breakthroughs in such new fields as resilience and mindfulness, emotional intelligence and social intelligence.

If we are indeed at a crossroads of consciousness, we might view the way ahead as branching off in two directions. Some researchers are calling our epoch the "Anthropocene" (following the Holocene). Human impact on Earth's biosphere now rivals previous natural agents of change, such as asteroid collision, advance of ice sheets, new species on the scene, and so on.

Our cognitive processes have now become planetary processes. And the hitch is that, while our self-awareness has given rise to outstanding cultural, scientific, and technical achievements, it's also spawned purposively deceptive propaganda, man-made natural disasters, the forced extinction of other species, genocide toward members of our own species, and so on. So, is our nonsustainable lifestyle throwing Mother Earth so out of balance that the time will come for human civilization to have to join the 99 percent of Earth's other, now-extinct species in saying, "Bye-bye"?

On the other hand, there's now research that views our Mother Earth as a living organism, dubbed "Gaia." Metaphorically, Gaia's *intention* is to optimize all life. In her interweaving of living and organic matter, we can see that diverse life forms and environments are coevolving, reciprocally. Avoiding extreme views on either side, might a middle way be seen if we can, as a species, awaken self-awareness of our responsibility to our environment? Are we just too nonadaptive to change, or can human nature live in harmony with Mother Nature? Coming home to ourselves in the present moment can include coming home to our roots in the ground of our being. A way to this harmonious path lies in our evolving awareness.

Mystic traditions have studied awareness for tens of thousands of years. Nondual philosopher Rupert Spira considers being aware of being aware like this: "The knowing of our being — or rather, awareness's knowing of its own being in us — is our primary experience, our most fundamental and intimate experience." Similarly, spiritual teacher Adyashanti expresses it thus:

> Each thought, feeling, and perception is
> occurring within a context of awareness.
> We are acknowledging there is this greater
> context of awareness and just by doing that
> the awareness is becoming conscious of itself.

Many are realizing this awareness of awareness for themselves through mindfulness. However we come to it, it brings us to a sense of our life as life itself, in natural kinship with all beings in mutual coemergence. ("Consider the lilies of the field . . . Even Solomon in all his glory was not arrayed like one of these" [Matthew 6:28–9].)

Ethically, awareness of awareness can reveal how self-awareness shapes our experience. This makes intention beautifully possible. Shaping a lifestyle shapes our lived world, including all who are in it, human and otherwise. Our ill- or well-being affects others, and vice-versa. Thus we can bend with the moral arc of the universe.

Awareness alone is not enough. Yet now, as a species, we're coming to know ourselves not just as individuals. This holds true at various levels of scale: as individuals, institutions, corporations, societies, nations, civilizations, and a species of earthlings. So I believe we're witnessing a new Great Turning. And awakening mindfulness is a key to that evolutionary spark.

So yet one more caption is possible for my brief incident on the epic bus of life: *What Does It Mean to Be Human?*

It's not the final caption by any means. Yet, from an evolutionary perspective, we're beginning to taste its meaning — in awakening, and awakening together. A tide is rising. Quietly, alongside the world's confusions and absurdities, outrages and indignities — a growing movement of contemplative practices is making spirituality personal and real in everyday life. More and more people are realizing engagement in the world as part of

© SAUL STEINBERG, *UNTITLED*, 1948

their personal development. Our evolution as a species, as well as individuals, can be conscious, and might well be the greatest game in town. As author and teacher Wes Nisker says, "Mindfulness is the opposable thumb of consciousness."

Q&A

Q *How do I practice mindfulness trainings?*

A I know people who carry them on a portable device and read them until their mind is clear. I read them every morning. I also turn to them when facing a dilemma and read them until my mind clears. At minimum, try reading all five aloud once a month, alone or in community.

You might also choose one training to study throughout the month (SOP). Practice being curious about yourself. Observe your everyday life in each training's clear, unflinching mirror. Observe how your thoughts, words, and deeds reflect your attitudes, and vice-versa. Notice where your aspirations find support and in what areas you feel resistance. Appreciate your strengths and vulnerabilities and how they interconnect. Stay focused on your core competencies and your evolutionary intentions; lead with love.

You might keep a journal. Because no one else will read it, you can let your words flow freely. Practice freewriting about a training: keep the pen moving as you note goals, obstacles, breakthroughs, and possibilities — and your attitudes toward them. Illustrate a training with pictures and poems, common sayings, and song lyrics. Consider whether your study of a training makes your daily meditation easier or fosters fresh insight and deeper understanding of reality.

Be aware of the reciprocity between self and others. What you recognize in yourself is true for others, and what you recognize in others is true for yourself. Let everyone you encounter be your teacher, your mirror, whether they're someone close to you, a clerk behind a counter, a difficult person in your life, a group of people, a cat yawning, a dog wagging a tail.

When life presents you with a mindfulness training to deal with, pause . . . breathe . . . smile . . . listen . . . study . . . learn.

Q *Do I have to take on all five trainings?*

A Good question. Work with what you feel comfortable with. Each training is interconnected with all the others. Practicing even just one deeply, you'll come to all the others.

If you don't believe me, consider this. There once was a mild-mannered, in-house accountant named Alfred.

Alfred had just one little bad habit. Once a month, he'd embezzle a small sum of money from the company. Deep down, Alfred knew better, but he preferred to lie to himself. He considered it merely a bit of white-collar crime. "Everybody does it, right?" he'd say to his conscience.

Well, eventually he grew nervous and began to drink to "steady his nerves." Then, one night, he went on a real bender. Staggering home, utterly smashed, he mistook his neighbor Joe's house for his. (This was in the suburbs, where the tract houses all look alike.) So our Alfred got into bed with Joe's wife. Joe, who worked the night shift, came home to find his wife in bed with another man, went berserk, and started calling the police. Terrified, Alfred raced into the kitchen, came back, and slayed Joe with a butcher knife. Theft ➤ lying ➤ intoxication ➤ adultery ➤ murder. End of story.

Q *I'd like to follow up on the previous question. Within any training, do I need to undertake all the parts?*

A This is a very interesting question. Being creative doesn't mean bending the guidelines to suit your fancy. On the other hand, please don't hang on to the words as if you're a trial attorney. Listen to their heart intentions. If you take on the trainings, do so because you want to live in a certain way, not because you're going to be rewarded or punished or monitored.

breathe

contemplation

lifestyle

worldview

WHAT IS LIFE? East and West join in agreement: breath is life. Dead people do not breathe. From our first breathing in, at birth, to our last breathing out, at death, life is one long now of breathing. Yet, of the 20,000 to 30,000 breaths we will draw today, of how many will we be conscious? Adding conscious breathing to our thinking, speaking, and acting — uniting mind-body-spirit as one — we *bloom*. In this way, every moment is an opportunity for living fully. With conscious breath as my constant companion . . . my mantra . . . my rosary . . . my continual prayer . . . I keep my appointment: my appointment with life.

what is meditation?

Feelings come and go like clouds in a windy sky.
Conscious breathing is my anchor.
THICH NHAT HANH

What is meditation? Please try this example out. While you're reading, be aware of your breathing. Once you've made that adjustment — being aware of breathing and aware of reading — see if you're more grounded, more able to *connect* personally to what you're reading, more available to digest whatever's especially true for you.

Good news! You can do this all the time! You can breathe while you sit, you can breathe while you walk.

You can breathe no matter where you are or what you're doing — in a car or in an elevator, washing a dish or waiting in line. You're breathing!

Our mind wanders, but our body's here and now, breathing. Conscious breathing can be our anchor. We can get dragged back into the past, which can lead to depression, or we can become anxious about the future, which can lead to fear. Conscious breathing returns us to the here and the now, where we really belong. It's a process requiring care, like training a horse: a slow learner in the beginning but, eventually, a champion.

I'll elaborate a bit on that in the following sections. As our centerpiece, I'll present Full Awareness of Breathing in depth. This practice can be seen as core to all three parts of this book. Plus, I'll introduce walking meditation and provide some final commentary and Q&A. But first — preparation.

PREPPING FOR FORMAL MEDITATION

Meditation's as simple as opening a fist. But simple isn't always easy. So it's good to prep before formal meditation to give it your best. It's similar to what you do when you first get into your car and run through a few preliminary rituals: Are the seat belts on? Is there enough gas? Is the emergency brake off? Do I have my directions? And so on.

First, pick a quiet spot with minimal distractions. Sit upright, in a relaxed but alert manner. Assume a posture that embodies, for you, awakened integrity and dignity.

If you're sitting in a chair, you have the option of scooting forward, away from the back of the chair, practicing self-reliance. If you can, you might also lift your hips up and tilt your pelvis back, sit back down, and see if your tailbone connects with your sit-space. (If your pelvis were a bowl, this means tilting the bowl back, so it doesn't spill forward.)

From there, see if you can stack your vertebrae up, so you're resting on your skeleton and using minimal muscles to hold yourself up. It's good to feel a three-pointed solidity, like the base of a pyramid, between your sit-space and feet flat on the floor if in a chair, or across sit-space and knees if you're on the ground. (If you're on the ground, you might feel more comfortable sitting on a cushion to make your knees lower than your pelvis.)

Everything from the waist down settles toward Mother Earth. Imagine your roots are going deep. From the waist up, you're aspiring toward the sky, like a tree. You might imagine that your head is a balloon: gently let it lift up your neck, sternum, and spine, letting them lengthen as they do so. Bring your head back: ears over shoulders. With your eyes parallel with the horizon, tuck your chin in and down just a bit. Let your skull sit balanced on its ring of bone, as free as a ping-pong ball atop a fountain.

Your eyes can be closed; if open, look toward a spot on the ground about a yard ahead, and gaze through that spot with soft eyes. Eyes open or closed, they're not getting distracted or attached to anything.

Lift your shoulders toward your ears, bring them back, and let them down. Let all your back muscles relax from your shoulders on down like a gentle waterfall. Bringing shoulder blades a bit closer together, allow your chest to open. If your elbows rest away from your torso, your ribs can expand as much as they wish. Your hands can rest on your knees or on your lap. Let your mind learn a lesson from your hands. When they're done with something, they put it down, done, and that's it. They're empty. Follow their good example: having let go, do nothing. Relax and rest.

Breathe through your nostrils. Plant your tongue on the roof of your mouth with the tip at the inside of your teeth or lip. Connecting the tongue and hard palate makes swallowing easier, joins vital energy channels (meridians) back and front, above and below, and helps silence mental chatter.* Nasal breathing has been promoted by energy masters and sages for thousands of years, and now scientists are discovering how it connects directly to the memory- and emotion-processing regions of our brain (the amygdala and hippocampus). Our sense of smell, even of just the freshness of air, reaches right to our soul.

All set. Ready? Go!

Sit still. Breathe. Smile.

---

*A Chinese folk proverb about silence teaches one to imagine speech as a valuable gold coin. Press it to the roof of your mouth. Do not let it slip away.

BASIC MEDITATION (ZEN)

Be still, and know.

PSALM 46:10

Welcome to the art of pausing. Be still, and know. All
the rest is commentary. Let your body and breath find
each other. Rest awareness in breathing. Place breath in
the foreground of consciousness. Let sensations, feelings, and thoughts come and go, off in the background,
without adding to them the least prejudice or judgment, label or story. They're just phenomena. They're
just out there. Let them come to you; you don't have
to go out to them. Merely notice as they arise, manifest, and pass away through your awareness, like breeze
through the open front and back doors of an empty
house. Don't cling to anything going by. Let phenomena wash over you while grounding deeply in open
awareness. Focusing on each breath and then the next,
silently observe perceptions, feelings, and thoughts as
they appear and vanish, like bubbles on a vast ocean of
attentive awareness.

If you wish, you might pause to compare the pace of
any verbal mind stream with the slower flow of breathing. Note how any residual roof-brain chatter seems
faster paced compared to breathing. Then you can
dial down the sound on the mental jukebox, shifting
attention back to your slower breathing. Quieting
the mind can be as simple as changing a radio station.

Tune the dial from Radio NST (nonstop talking) to commercial-free TNT (think: nonthinking). As John Lennon suggests, "Turn off your mind, relax, and float downstream . . . "

Those are sample guidelines for a basic meditation sometimes known as Zen.* The word means "meditation": choiceless attention, open awareness.

No agenda.

Effortless.

Be still, and know. It's a venerable and vital tradition, for good reason. To do anything, it's important to be able to do nothing. And to understand why. To be conscientious about it, consider making space for it in your home: find your breathing room. It could even be on your bed. Take time for it within your everyday routine. Ideally, formal practice might be a twenty-minute meditation when you first get out of bed and/or a twenty-minute session before going to bed. I do both. Eventually, you might make this the center of one day a week, a Day of Mindfulness (a.k.a. "Sabbath"). Over time, you'll come to know your mind. You'll also become acquainted with subtle and potent states of consciousness, a spectrum of awakening, the gamut of what it means to be alive.

---

*It's noteworthy that Thich Nhat Hanh is fairly unique in teaching both the Zen and mindfulness schools of meditation. Geography partly explains it. Traditional mindfulness is practiced in South/Southeast Asia (India, Sri Lanka, Thailand, Myanmar, Laos, Cambodia). Zen is practiced in East Asia (China, Korea, Japan). Vietnam is located in between the two. (In Vietnam, Zen is called Thien [pronounced "teen"].)

Informally, this could be a way of nurturing our instinctive capacity for wellness, which is another word for wholeness. (What exercise is to fitness, meditation is to wellness.) Self-care/self-healing: all it takes is pausing . . . breathing . . . and becoming intimate with our own life. Zen meditation can be as regular as the sunrise, as personal as a fingerprint, or as cosmic as realizing the universe contemplates itself in us. All perfectly natural.

Be still and know.

MINDFUL ZEN/ZEN MINDFULNESS

In my weekly mindfulness practice group, we often sit for twenty minutes in open silence: Zen. Other times, we anchor our sit with a semi-guided meditation, for focused mindfulness. Both modes foster awakening. As in cross-training, each complements the other.

Zen is a matter of accepting anything experienced, fixing on no particular object, remaining aware of awareness. It doesn't have any particular pattern. Yet, over time, one notices certain landmarks. For instance, the following phases of experience mark, for me, the rough outline of an average Zen sit: settling down . . . getting into a groove . . . noticing what's particular today . . . deepening . . . letting go and being vulnerable and present.

In mindfulness, we might direct our attention to distinct phases of awareness, such as the following, which we'll explore next:

Awakening mindfulness of breath
Concentration
Calming
Gladdening
Gratitude

Sitting silently in Zen, we'd notice these phases eventually. Mindfulness singles out such key elements, arranging them like beads on a string, for discerning study. No one phase is better or higher than any other. As St. Catherine of Siena tells us, "All the way to heaven is heaven."

full awareness of breathing

In the heritage of mindfulness, there's a foundational meditation practice. While it comes to us from across two-and-a-half millennia, it's still flower-fresh. It's called Full Awareness of Breathing. Please note: This isn't about taking deep, full breaths, as in yoga. Rather, it's about full awareness: grounded in the present moment, living fully. How? By centering our awareness on our breathing.

Full Awareness of Breathing is practiced by millions around the planet, in Zen, mindfulness, and other traditions. Our version has been handcrafted by Thich

Nhat Hanh*. If PBS makes up a fifty-second meditation, Full Awareness of Breathing can form the basis
for an in-depth, *formal* meditation. Beginners often
struggle to sit still for more than five or ten minutes.
Here, spending four minutes on each phase, you have a
twenty-minute meditation; a done deal. It can be practiced even longer, for forty minutes or for hours. Once
you are familiar with it, you can do a speed-through in
just a few minutes. It can be accessed at home alone or
with a facilitator in a group — or right now, breathing
and reading.

The setup is akin to the mindfulness verses. We focus
our breath and full awareness on pairs of images, with
each line summed up by a key word. For example:

Breathing in, I know I am breathing in.   [in]
Breathing out, I know I am breathing out.   [out]

In is the key word for the first line, and *out* is the key
word for the second.

---

* Full Awareness of Breathing is one of two essential, traditional texts on mindfulness. When
Thich Nhat Hanh first discovered it, he said, "I felt I was the happiest person in the world,"
and he has been teaching it ever since. Forty years ago, he introduced his translation of
the original text in *The Miracle of Mindfulness*, and twenty years later, he published it with
his commentary in a book titled *Breathe, You Are Alive!* Soon after, he taught the five-part
version. Then, at retreats from 2007–2014, he went over the text's four sets of four practices.
He later published a chart of those sixteen practices in *No Mud, No Lotus*.

Its companion foundational mindfulness text is The Four Frames of Mindfulness (body,
feelings, mind, and reality). It intertwines with Full Awareness of Breathing and will form
the basis of the sequel to this book.

I'll start with the guidelines. Then I'll share an expanded version, with commentary, interpretation, and additional teachings. You can always discover new layers of meaning and application.

The basic outline as Thich Nhat Hanh teaches it goes like this:

1   Breathing in, I know   [in]
        I am breathing in.
    Breathing out, I know   [out]
        I am breathing out.

2   Breathing in, I notice my   [deep]
        breath has become deep.
    Breathing out, I notice my [slow]
        breath has become slow.

3   Breathing in, I calm my body [calm]
        and my mind.
    Breathing out, I feel at ease. [ease]

4   Breathing in, I smile.   [smile]
    Breathing out, I release.   [release]

5   Breathing in, I go back   [present moment]
        to the present moment.
    Breathing out, I know this [wonderful moment]
        is a wonderful moment.

Our job is only to be aware of our in-breath and nothing else; then our out-breath and nothing else. Breathing in, we focus on the first line, and breathing out we focus on the second line. Then, once we've settled into it, we can say to ourselves just the key word: for example, *in* with our inhale, *out* with our exhale. We might elongate the key word to fit the measure of our breath: *iiiin . . . owwwwwt.* Or mentally repeat it like a soft bell: *in . . . in . . . in . . . out . . . out . . . out.*

When we coordinate our words with our breathing, we allow our spirit, body, and mind to come together as one. The pairs of lines and then their key words serve as cues for your awareness until they *become* your awareness. Once you get it, and feel fully settled into it, then you can let go of the words. You'll know when you get there. Rest in your awareness of breathing like a bird swaying softly on the gently undulating surface of a calm ocean.

Each of the five phases can take from five to fifteen breaths each. After feeling fulfilled by one pair of phrases, please move ahead to the next pair and then their key words and then silent, open awareness.

IN, OUT . . . DEEP, SLOW

This grand meditation is quite easy to memorize. The key words make a kind of poem:

> In, Out
> Deep, Slow
> Calm, Ease

Smile, Release
Present Moment, Wonderful Moment

This can also be sung.

It doesn't matter if you don't think you sing well. In and of itself, singing can stimulate and regularize the breath, while focusing the mind on a few simple, meaningful points instead of 10,000 scattered thoughts. If you're singing together with a group of friends, "sing with your ears": loud enough to hear your voice seamlessly as part of a chorus, but not as loud as a soloist against a back-up choir. It always inspires me when it feels as if a community is coming out of everyone's mouth, my own included, a voice of common humanity. I feel like a drop of water flowing as a river.

Singing is a universal reminder to celebrate life. Don't be like one of those two-leggeds about whom the birds in

In, Out, Deep, Slow

Words by Thich Nhat Hanh

Music by Chân Hoa Lâm

In, out. Deep— slow. Calm, ease. Smile, re - lease.

Pres - ent mo - ment. Won - der - ful mo - ment.

the trees gossip: "There goes that sad species without any time to ever just sing and dance!"

COMMENTARY

There are literally hundreds of commentaries on Full Awareness of Breathing. With this addition to the record, I'm also sharing my own report of some findings from along the way. Feel free to pick up one or two comments and see if they shine for you, like travelers' lights on a forest trail at night. Remember: there's no "right way" to meditate. There's only your way. As you grow more familiar with meditation it can teach you more about itself, sort of the way a cat can teach you how to play with it. Trust intuition. Engage creativity. Unlearn useless and pointless knowledge. Relearn the common *knowing* that's part of the collective consciousness shared by mountains and rivers, penguins and bees, tides and whispering pines.

our constant companion
conscious breathing

| Breathing in, I know I am breathing in. | [in] |
| Breathing out, I know I am breathing out. | [out] |

Begin here. Put everything else on pause . . . and awaken mindfulness of breathing.

Notice the breath in your nostrils. Identify an in-breath, as an in-breath. Identify an out-breath, as an out-breath. Let the rhythm of verbal thought be replaced by the rhythm of breathing.

One word after another is replaced by one breath after another. This is a different way of doing: we're merely being. Be your breath. First, recognize you're breathing. And pay attention. Observe the beginning, middle, and end of an in-breath and the beginning, middle, and end of an out-breath. Mindfully, you can discern, too, a slight pause between an in-breath and the next out-breath, and another slight pause between an out-breath and the next in-breath.

Mindfully aligned, feel your breath and body and mind *flow* as one.

BREATH, OUR ORIGINAL TEACHER

Pause . . . breathe . . . smile. It's phenomenal, indeed. With conscious breathing we can release ourselves from the control of our autonomic nervous system (our reptilian brain) that's been breathing unconsciously. We can breathe as if opening our eyes to see for ourselves that it's a new day! We connect with life, however it might be, more fully, more deeply.

We grow aware of ourselves as a species of mammal capable of being conscious of our consciousness. That is, paying attention to breath, we also awaken our awareness. We're not only watching our breath, we're being *watchful*. With just one conscious breath, mindful awareness can awaken instantly, permeating our consciousness. Mind becomes one with its object, so making life-giving breath the object of our mind it becomes our mind.

Isn't that worth a smile?

Smile at your in-breath. Smile at your out-breath.

Congratulations! You've inherited the world's greatest wealth: the awareness of being alive! Just by paying attention, we're bazillionaires of breath. Our mindfulness of breathing is investing us in a reserve of subtle, serene, intense, kindly, intelligent alertness we can always bank on. And we never have to be tight-fisted skinflints about our wealth because awareness compounds interest. There's a natural law of abundance: it's regenerative. Mere air proves more precious than all the gold hidden in vaults. Everyone could be rewarded just for breathing.

Be a trailblazer. Set up your tent today in a world of values beyond money.

Don't delay. Enjoy your priceless inheritance of awakening right away.

This is absolutely marvelous. When we are aware of our breathing, we discover mindfulness isn't about any generic, off-the-shelf, ready-made, one-size-fits-all type of breathing . . . it's not any *kind* of breathing at all. It's free from any "methods" of breathing, such as "breath*work*." How liberating! This is the method of No Method. Let breath itself be our teacher. As it is. Just so. Moment to moment.

We can experience what it means to merely observe. We don't control our breath; we just observe it. This also means learning to relinquish the urge to control life. We learn, instead, to accept and go along with how things are.

We also learn to stop "concepting" (wishing, narrating, judging). We're involved instead with actual life-giving breath in our nostrils . . . right now . . . manifesting its own unique, most particular in and out. We're right there as it happens within awakening awareness.

mindful body / embodied mind
quality time

Breathing in, I notice my breath   [deep]
     has become deep.
Breathing out, I notice my breath   [slow]
     has become slow.

Awareness awakens when attention is focused on breath's coming and going at our nostrils. This awareness can expand to include the whole body breathing and bringing our mind the gift of undivided attention.

YOUR FOCUS: LIGHT, FIRM, STRONG, EASY, AND FREE
To awaken, pay attention.

It's that simple. Wherever we are, whatever we're doing, we always have our breath as focus for our attention. Please give it your utmost attention. Our breath's been our inner teacher since birth. In humble silence I heed it and follow.

When our mind wanders (that's when, not if), as soon as we've noticed, we gently return our awareness to our breath. And smile. Mind-wandering isn't failure. Observing it is an important part of getting to know our mind. That too is part of contemplation.

We dwell in a culture saturated by electronic media. This can bring us wonderful things. Yet it can come at the price of the hacking of our attention. I hope your average attention span isn't like the crow's, always distracted by any shiny flashing that might prove to be a juicy beetle. Meditation trains us in one-pointed concentration, so we're fully aware of what's in front of our nose, and nothing else; in this case, our breath and ourselves in our environment.

Since we're not controlling our breath, nothing need feel forced, as in concentrating for a test. There's no tension at all. Mindful attention's as light as a butterfly, yet strong as an ox, free as a cloud and easy as drinking a cup of tea. It's an *absorption*, as is doing anything we love.

ONE-POINTED VISUALIZATIONS

Focusing our attention on our breathing can awaken a marvelous one-pointed concentration. To train in that, here are three traditional visualizations.

1 Imagine your nostrils are the gates of a castle. You are installed inside the gates as a sentry. Your duty is to pay attention to only the comings and goings of breath at the gates, not to try to track any further activity past your post, neither inside the inner castle nor outside in the world beyond. Only comings in and goings out.

2 Imagine your breath is a saw. Be aware of the entirety of your in-breath and out-breath as being like the upstroke and downstroke of sawing a log. You're paying total attention to the even line where the saw teeth are entering and leaving the log.

3 The sheer physics of breathing is fantastic. The Lung Institute informs us that if our lungs were open flat they'd cover the size of a tennis court. To let that sink in, appreciate the anatomy of breathing through further visualization. Imagine our lungs function like a bellows. Visualize as you breathe how, when our diaphragm flexes downward, air is drawn into our lungs, from the upper lobes on down. When our diaphragm relaxes, air passes out of our lungs from the bottom up.

For further concentration, notice where your body makes contact with breathing. From your pores to your bones. From your scalp to your toes. It's good to move beyond breathing in our ribs only. That can make for shallow breathing, such as babies do when they're tense. Soften the belly, our vital physical and energetic center. Allow the abdomen to expand and contract with breath.

Relaxing, expanded belly.

Relaxing, expanded mind.

CONCENTRATION IS MEDITATION

If you give complete attention with your body, with your nerves, with your eyes, with your mind, with your whole being, there is no center from which you are attending, there is only attention. That attention is complete silence.

J. KRISHNAMURTI

When we are grounded in awareness of breathing, we're establishing a base for a single-pointed concentration that is, itself, meditation. Mindful concentration frees us from playing out mere concepts about our life, so we can live life fully as it is here and now. We're also reminded that machines multitask well, but people don't. We read while we eat (double the consumption). But each act involves separate bodily systems. Jammed together, neither reading nor eating gets done efficiently. Even if we're only eating, we rarely chew a single mouthful. Instead, we're forking in the next bite before we've even swallowed the first. One-pointed concentration means that if we're eating an orange, we do so one slice at a time. Communing with the whole universe in the orange, slice by slice.

So why not treat our breathing (and everything else) the same way?

Concentration, in and of itself, can awaken us. Given prolonged attention to breath, a shift in our psychic base can occur. Everything's no longer all about me: my likes, my dislikes, my possessions, my résumé. We can leave that stark, simplistic, abstract, fantasy realm, always dominated by our desires — and aversions, which are only the flipside of the same self-absorption — to discover reality, rich in nuance, subtlety, texture, ever-changing like a music.

This shift in awareness can be a gradual awakening, over time, but you might mark how it can happen spontaneously in the space of just a smile . . . a pause . . . a breath. And the more we enjoy this fundamental shift of attention, the more readily we might choose it. For example, we might ask ourselves if we notice a shift in pace and depth.

SLOWING DOWN, GROWING DEEP

Newcomers to mindfulness are often amazed, sometimes even shocked, to discover how busily their minds can race and that they've never been aware of this before. It's like gazing down at a clear stream, admiring all the smooth stones lining the stream bed, when, unexpectedly, a little leaf falls upon the surface then *whoosh!*

zooms away. The leaf surprises us by showing how swiftly a current has been flowing invisibly. So too can our mind race like the wind, without our realizing it.

Newcomers are then equally impressed to discover how their mind can *slow* on its own. Breath too. Meditation encourages that natural facility. When you feel a slowing of breath and mind, pause, acknowledge it appreciatively (smile) — and pay attention. You're not trying to change anything. (If you were then who's the horse and who's the rider?) Rather, you're witnessing, with a gentle, humble curiosity, how a slower pace emerges on its own. In an ever-accelerating culture, this can be a huge relief. Looking around, we recognize how nature tends to move: slow- and medium-paced, with occasional fast bursts. So going slow feels good and is perfectly natural. To verify and explore this further, as an experiment in awakening mindfulness, try going about your daily activities aware of your breathing while also doing everything just a little bit slower.

I also pause and smile when I notice my breath has grown *deep*. How profound and right this depth feels! It's quite different from today's superficial culture that skims over everything like a bunch of ants scampering upon a watermelon without ever tasting it. I also remind myself that this depth is without need of the architecture of intellectual fabrication. An empty sky is immeasurably profound. As is a bird, a tree, the earth beneath my feet.

HOW DEEP IS THE OCEAN?

Slowed down, we become more aware of possibilities of depth — depth of breath, mind, heart, and soul. As these aspects of ourselves come together we grow more deeply centered and grounded. With breath as our primary object of attention, our awareness can let go of any other object for it to attach itself to. Freed awareness can then even reflect upon itself — being aware of being aware. Deep awareness plus subtle discernment can be called full awareness. Whether or not we experience this unlimited heart-mind always, it's certainly good to touch deeply from time to time.

We might think meditation is listening to the Source . . . and prayer is speaking to the Source. Mindful breathing clarifies that it's both. Beyond petition or plea. "Absolutely unmixed attention is prayer," attests Simone Weil. And Thomas Merton confesses, "How I pray is breathe." This isn't so much theology as a working recipe for good nourishment and potent medicine.

Some people pray by invoking a mantra or the name of an angel or an aspect of the Ultimate; practitioners of mindfulness might mentally recite the words *in* and *out*. Some people use beads to count prayers; students of mindfulness use beads to focus on breath, each bead marking a round of in and out. Do such mindfulness practices exhibit any less devotion? Mindful of our breathing, we are filled with Holy Spirit. There's more than enough to go around.

BECOME A CONNOISSEUR OF AIR

Here's another marvelous shift. So often we base our
life on quantities, such as time, distance, money, and so
on. Instead, this is *quality* time. Centered on awareness
of breath, we can discover the diversity of qualities in
ourselves and within life. You might find yourself falling
into an intimate dialogue with breath, as between old
friends. "Hello, my dear breath! Are you swift today, or
slow? Shallow, or deep? Audible, or silent? Are you a bit
jagged and bumpy like a river? Are you sort of tumbly,
like a little waterfall? Or, are you silky smooth as a wide,
shallow stream flowing over fine sand?" What we notice
in our breath is also present in our sensations, feelings,
and mind — and the universe.

Contemplation of qualities helps develop an inquiring
mind. A valuable trait. Why not grow curious about life?
As if threading beads of breath on a string, we can hold
each new bead up to the light of impartial mindfulness
and relish its unique quality. Pace. Depth. Shape. Speed.
Nuance. Texture. Feeling.

— Notice what you notice.

CONCENTRATION AND AWAKENING

Alert and discerning, we can appreciate how dynamic
our mindfulness can become. Our breath deepens.
Our concentration deepens. Our meditation deepens.
They condition each other. Meditation, concentration, and breath are not separate. Rather, they interact,
and inter-react. Together, they fuel the energy of

mindfulness, which has the power to fully awaken us. So paying good attention can yield invaluable boons, Awakening being the best of all. Whatever we call it — Awakening, Enlightenment, Liberation, Salvation — transformation of consciousness is the ultimate goal of many great paths of spiritual seeking. Yet, to our way of seeing, Awakening often simply just happens. We can't make it happen. (That would be like trying to bite our own teeth.) Awakening can occur more like an accident. The good news is: mindfulness can make us accident-prone.

Zen tradition is full of wonderful dramatic vignettes of spiritual seekers awakening to Ultimate Reality, spontaneously, and in the oddest moments: walking to the teacher's cottage, dropping a teapot, and witnessing it shattering . . . sweeping a porch and hearing a pebble strike a hollow stalk of bamboo . . . seeing a tree near a friend's front door as if for the first time . . . or hearing a bird squawk, overhead and in one's own mind, at the same time. It's not that the teapot or the pebble, the tree or the bird *cause* Awakening. Awakened mind is always present. Rather, shoring up reserves of concentration provides fertile ground for the seeds of Awakening to blossom.

Sitting still, following our breath, absorbed in qualities within experience of awareness, we come to know a calm mind . . . which ushers us through the next gateway.

peace is every breath
a satisfied mind

> Breathing in, I calm my body and my mind.   [calm]
> Breathing out, I feel at ease.   [ease]

Maybe we've *tried* to quiet our mind and found it like trying to chase our own tail. It can be quite a marvelous surprise to discover how our mind can calm on its own. Sitting still, resting in full awareness of breath, we might feel a quiet, calm ease. We might feel our whole body as calmed and our mind too. We might note how our body-breath and mind-heart can align without being told to. We might have a sense of stability and tranquility — stable as a mountain; calm as a forest pool in early dawn; still as a pebble at the bottom of that lake.

Note: this isn't self-hypnosis. Calm is already present within each of us. No one has to manufacture it or search for it. When we're no longer layering our experience with judgments and storylines, we find this calm is very much part of who we truly are, down deep. We've always known how to do this, but somehow just plain forgot. It's an aspect of our true nature, our wise inner teacher, our constant companion whom we've so often neglected. So it can be wonderful to just be ourselves for a change. (Actually, you might as well be yourself: everyone else is taken.)

PEACE, THE FRUITION OF MINDFULNESS

An out-breath (carbon dioxide) nourishes the trees; trees' exhalation (oxygen) nourishes us. Full awareness of breathing can awaken us to this vaster field of awareness, attuned to the rhythm of all that is alive: the pulse of the heart and the ocean's tides, the dance of sun and moon, the wheel of the changing seasons. In contemplation, we often come to feel as if breath itself is breathing. As if we're *being breathed*. If we had to give it a name, what might we call this ease of breathing, feeling centered, grounded in a silent, clear, spacious, natural sense of calm?

Peace!

Touching peace. Dwelling in peace. Being peace. This surpasses any concept of peace. "Peace . . . passeth all understanding" (Philippians 4:7). This may seem esoteric, but it's actually quite sensible. It's one thing to know the *name* of a flower; it's another thing to *know* a flower. (Hello, red rose!) A direct experience of peace naturally follows a moment-to-moment opening to qualities of breath. Going beyond qualities, we dwell in their ground of being. We genuinely appreciate life without qualification, unconditionally, in unobstructed awareness.

We feel peace in ourselves, peace in our family, peace in the world, peace of mind.

Have you met your mind yet? It's a key component of our operating system which, however, lacks a precious owner's manual. Yet mind is our basic interface, the container for our experience, the mirror of our heart.

For one thing, our mind can operate as a receiver but also a transmitter. An agitated, unconscious mind perceives everything as trouble, like a monkey running through a dry forest with its tail on fire, setting it all ablaze and freaking out at the growing inferno all around, which it is causing. But mind can serve us well, just like a monkey can be trained to be our ally in the wilderness. An awakened, self-aware mind can nourish wholesome, happy experiences. In alignment with our body and our heart, mind has almost limitless potential for remarkable healing and transformation.

Being engaged in keen, relaxed concentration, the mind naturally settles, no longer scattered like dandelion seeds in the wind. It grows tranquil. Peaceful. Such a serene mind is like a mirror reflecting whatever's in front of it, just as it is, like a vast, flat lake reflecting a blue sky. Thoughts, feelings, and perceptions come and go — and mind just observes them, like clouds, evaporating in the bright, warm sun of dawning awareness. In deep meditation, it can also seem as if the mind's reflecting practically no thing whatsoever. Or everything. A calm mind is capable of boundless awareness. No longer mirroring fears or fantasies, a clear mind vividly reflects What Is. Such a mind of peace is a priceless treasure, indeed.

Grounded in sheer awareness . . . dwelling in calm, silent peace . . . we pass through a fourth gateway, marked "Gladness."

relaxing and gladdening
this is a happy moment

Breathing in, I smile.   [smile]
Breathing out, I release.   [release]

Peace is like coming home. It's as if, at the end of a long day at work, you've come through your door and feel a friendly wave of warmth washing all through you. You have arrived, you're home: in the here and in the now. *This* is a happy moment!

TRUE HAPPINESS

Joy manifests spontaneously. Just like that. The fact is, we're glad just to be alive. We forget this when we're always running. Once we remember, and reconnect with our natural gladness, it's good to sit with it from time to time. This is restorative. We might also feel then how there's a happiness that runs deeper beneath this exuberant zest for life. This happiness isn't some passing pleasure or some smiley cartoon. True happiness is bedrock. It's prolonged depression that is unnatural; Soul is inherently buoyant and light. The Declaration of Independence even declares happiness is everyone's inherent and inalienable birthright: our true nature.

MOUTH YOGA

There's reason enough for quiet rejoicing. After all, what good is meditation, or peace, or awakening if you don't enjoy it?! What's your motivation? Like all beings, we want to be happy. So, right now, why not give yourself the gift of a smile?

Smiling is empowering, in and of itself. Here's a simple, fifty-second practice some call "mouth yoga." It goes like this. Lift just one corner of your mouth very lightly in a faint smile. Hold it for a round of three breaths. How does it feel? Try it out six times a day. In just a few days, you might notice a difference in body and mind. I find it similar to a bell of mindfulness. First I half-smile then relax all the fifty or so other muscles of my face. (A full smile uses about twelve, but a half-smile just two.) Focusing on just that one spot, breath by breath, I relax and release any tension in all my body's muscles, nerves, feelings, heart, mind. As Thich Nhat Hanh reminds us, sometimes joy precedes a smile, but sometimes a smile precedes the joy. So if our body can produce a chemistry of happiness,* why be prejudiced against our body?

JUST A FAINT SMILE CAN MOVE THE NEEDLE

A member of my mindfulness circle also attends a "laughter yoga" workshop. But never underestimate the power of a simple smile. It not only affects happiness but also

---

*In 1974, scientists discovered that the human body produces its own internal, feel-good chemistry. They named the chemicals *endorphins*, combining two Greek roots: Morpheus, the god of dreams, after whom morphine is named, and *éndon*, meaning "from within."

our general attitude toward being alive. And we can direct a mindful smile both inward and outward. Greeting my heart with an in-breath, smiling to my heart as I breathe out, I sense my pulse. Noticing a lovely cloud going by in the sky, I gaze up at the cloud as I inhale. As I exhale, I smile at the cloud. After a couple breaths, I sense the cloud revealing herself more intimately. This intimacy also pertains to me, as my eyes are a watery medium, not to mention my body being more than half water, so what I see in the watery cloud reflects my own wateriness.

This kind of conversation doesn't require Wi-Fi or a phone. Wherever we are, we can pause, smile, and enjoy a silent dialogue with life anytime at all, within and all around. Mouth yoga can also be superb for releasing tension, stress, or pain. For example, sitting in meditation, I can neutralize an itch with just three mindful breaths. Smile, just noting the itch but not scratching.

With that as a model, so too can we locate and release physical, emotional, and mental kinks and knots. Scanning your body with your breath, note where you find withholding, constriction, pain . . . in your mind, your feelings, your body. If you can locate a node of tension with your in-breath . . . breathe into it, smiling hello to it. Connecting with it. Then, with your out-breath . . . relax and release, letting it go. It's as if our mindful smile is like a heat lamp, capable of unknotting cramped muscles, gnarly emotions, and tangled mind formations beneath its warm, healing, penetrative radiance. Pause, smile, breathe, release.

I remember learning to deal with pain during a heat wave. Growing up in Los Angeles, whenever the weather broke 100°F, I'd try to ignore the discomfort, but to no avail. Yet I couldn't just dial another station. And people around me were so crabby, I didn't want to be like them. So one day I stopped identifying with heatwave fatigue and my attitudes about it. Instead, I smiled at the heat, embraced the heat, experiencing it fully, melting into it. I observed where I felt it in my body, feelings, and mind, released my attitudinal concepts, and just went with the flow of the heat wave. I learned the meaning of "It is what it is." As it becomes evident when we abandon desire and aversion and opt for moment-to-moment awareness of breath, I found the heat as no longer a fixed, plain red stripe across my consciousness, but rather truly an ever-changing wave. Once I found my balance and got into my own rhythm with it, I discovered heat waves as a good occasion for celebrating creative activities, like writing, drawing, or dancing.

Breathing in and gladdening — breathing out and letting go of whatever doesn't nourish comfort, happiness, care, and love — we learn to discard much needless suffering.

LOOKING DEEPLY AND RELEASING

With stability and calm, we can look deeply. For instance, when you encounter physical, emotional, or mental obstacles — pause, breathe, smile, and "name it to tame it." Call it out by name, whatever it might be. Say, "Stress." "Anxiety." "Self-doubt." "Envy." "Spite." This could also mean mentally identifying its root or its effect — "rehears-ing" . . . "judging" . . . "tightness" . . . "dry mouth" . . . "butterflies in stomach."

Name the difficulty on the in-breath. Smile at it (and your attitude toward it) with the out-breath. Give it a couple more breaths to see if it reveals itself more fully. Notice if energy moves in your body awareness. With each out-breath, watch to see if it resolves . . . and dissolves like morning dew. When you name something, you're already coming to terms with it. Neuroscience teaches us a neat trick to this. Verbalization moves diffi-cult energy from the more primitive parts of our brain to the executive parts where, caught in the act, it holds less sway and can be more easily neutralized.

If the challenge still remains, consider it an ally in disguise, a messenger, a teacher. Honor the resistance. Sometime later, when you're in a stabilized, serene medita-tion, circle back. Bring the persistent obstacle to mind, and the feeling. Sit with it in a friendly manner, in dialogue, smiling at its manifestation, and get to know it better. What's its energy . . . shape . . . color . . . sound . . . taste? What sensations or feelings seem associated with it? Where do you feel it in your body? What memories does it evoke? What triggers it? What's your attitude toward it? What's at stake if you just let it go, right now? See what insights arise.

Then . . . gently . . . drop it. (All of it.) Move on.

Something similar may return, but maybe next time in a tamer version. Don't worry. It's already become a part of you. Now you're coming to know it better. You don't have to push it away or fight it. The fly finds its way out of the empty bottle the same way it got in. Simply leave the door open for it.

I can sum up this fourth phase of Full Awareness of Breathing with the game of Catch and Release. It's easy. Let yourself *be breathed*. Let air just fall into your lungs (*accept, catch!*). Smile at wherever you feel contact with breath. Then release any knot where you feel you're holding back or that's holding you back. Do the same for feelings and thoughts. Let the knot fall away along with the air from your lungs (*let go, release!*) as far as the horizon. Repeat as often as necessary.

And be glad you're playing this game on *this* side of the grass.

an attitude of gratitude
i have enough —
and more than enough

Breathing in, I go back   [present moment]
    to the present moment.
Breathing out, I know this   [wonderful moment]
    is a wonderful moment.

(For key words here I sometimes use *now* / *wow!* or *now* / *and how!*)

When asked what time it is, beloved baseball player Yogi Berra would answer, "You mean now?" In his honor, I've replaced the twelve numbers on the dial of my office clock with just the word *now*. To connect our awareness with the present moment is to touch a plane of experience where space and time are relative. Wherever we go, we're always *here*. Whenever we're there, it's always *now*. In reality, loving awareness has no beginning, middle, end, or fixed location.

With this expansive awareness, we can step away from any meditation prompts we've used and just experience our life, as is, right now — as we sit in the center of our lives . . . appreciatively vulnerable to whatever's happening . . . intimately connected to life itself. (Come as you are.) We've come full circle, arriving where we began: finding ourselves at our own door — our true home, in the here and in the now — with an attitude of gratitude now for the simplest things of life, each a miracle.

THANKS GIVING

> Concentration and contemplation are great things;
> but no contemplation is greater than the life
> we have about us every day.
> HAZRAT INAYAT KHAN

Each of us can count ourselves lucky to have time to do absolutely nothing but *be*. (After all, we're human *be*-ings.) As we complete our formal sitting, we have a wonderful chance to take stock. As poet Lawson Fusao Inada asks, "Where's the list of things *not* to be grateful for?" Any time of day or night, you might pause and make a mental list of what you might feel grateful for. Right now, I am grateful for the support of Mother Earth, my warm body freely breathing, eyes that can see the blue sky, the coolness of a breeze from the Pacific through my window caressing my face and empty hands, ears that can hear birds, a neighbor's baby burbling.

In taking stock, I also list what else I might take for granted: being alive, a roof over my head, food to eat, friends. Thich Nhat Hanh notes, "Many people are alive but don't touch the miracle of being alive." And it's miraculous to rediscover this, daily. We need only pause, breathe, and smile to witness, enjoy, and engage the wonders of life. It's healthy and empowering to be grateful, aware there are enough causes and conditions for being happy in the present moment.

completion

When our sit is complete, we don't look at our watch, say, "OK, I'm done!" and go skipping away. True, some people have a way of going from meditation into whatever's next without skipping a beat. Maybe they're Zen practitioners of nonattainment/nonmeditation. Yet some kind of closure could be helpful. It's like when we've baked a cake and take it out of the oven: if it's not properly set, *ploof!* the whole thing can collapse. Similarly, we can take a few moments to let our meditation set. We let its goodness get fully absorbed into our mind-body, so it doesn't leak away and we can easily access it later. This could also be an excellent time for the meditation of setting intention. We can also soak up what it means to say, "I have enough." Complete.

SOAK THE SIT: TAKING IN THE GOOD

There's no one set way to meditate nor to complete a meditation. We can be creative. Sufi mystic Rumi speaks of this when he says, "There are hundreds of ways to kneel and kiss the ground." Joining palms and bowing is one of the simplest formal ways of opening and of completing a sit. Some think of one hand as *body* and the other hand as *mind* and join them. Others consider joined palms to be an act of letting go — and feeling connected.

You might observe the light upon your hands, then on the floor, then in the room. Notice if you see and feel more nuance, texture, vividness, shapeliness, *space*.

Some soak their sit by practicing lovingkindness (a.k.a. *metta*) meditation. Since this has become widely known, I'll conclude our tour of the Full Awareness of Breathing with Taking in the Good instead. Here's how I practice it.

I place one palm on my heart region, in the center of my chest. Closing my eyes, I breathe in the goodness I'm feeling in the present moment. With each inhale, I reflect upon the wholesome nourishment my meditation has given me. On each exhale, I open my heart in gratitude. I take all this good into my heart, feeling it there beneath my palm holding it in. And, after five or ten or fifteen breaths, I regard how this feels for future reference.

Then I put my other palm over the back of the hand on my heart. To this mixture of feelings of immediately present good that I'm holding on to, I now add additional factors that came together to enable this goodness to manifest (teachers, family, friends, livelihood). Breathing in / *goodness*, breathing out / *gratitude*.

After several breaths taking in this now-multiplied goodness, taking note of how it feels, and massaging it into my heart with both hands, I add to the mix the goodness of nonobvious factors that enabled the obvious factors (anything and everything — the farmer who grew my breakfast cereal, the trucker who brought it to a warehouse, their spouses and families, the sun that shone on it all, the rain, the roads). With my palms upon my expanding heart center, I allow my heart to overflow.

I'll remain in this space until I feel the goodness seeping into the marrow of my bones, permeating every molecule of my soul. I set positive intentions. And throughout the day I might pause to remind myself how this openhearted goodness is a natural fact, our inherent, true nature.

There's no formula for completing a meditation. Some people just let go of meditation and just move on. What's important is realizing how everything can be a point of contact for meditation. It's as continuous as a circle. Engaging each thing fully, each moment is complete, and the circle is ever unbroken.

formal and informal mindfulness, same difference

I often use the Full Awareness of Breathing template for a *formal*, twenty- to forty-minute sit. Being already familiar with it in my bones, I can tap into it with a couple breaths for each of the five stages, for a shorter, *informal* session. I begin by being aware of breath in my nostrils. I then expand awareness to my whole body breathing. This enables me to calm body and mind, which leads to joy and letting go. Then I experience fully what it means to be alive. Informal practice finds life's daily concerns as the object of mindfulness. Formal and informal are two sides of the same coin, like long and short, and I recommend both.

Formal practice can mean devoting time to touch deeply, twenty to forty minutes, say. Sitting still for a length of time lets our body clue in to the fact we're not going anywhere, not doing anything, so it can turn off our instinctual fight, flight, or freeze mode and allow more evolved states of consciousness to emerge. I liken formal practice to boring straight down, right from where you are, and digging a well. Then you don't have to draw from anyone else's aquifer. You're being self-reliant. With practice, you're always adding to your reservoir, from the source. It then becomes easier to fall into profound, formal meditation. And you can draw from the depths of this well throughout the day through everything you do (and don't do) as informal meditation.

Informal practice is like the mortar that holds the bricks of formal practice together. Informal mindfulness is the practice of touching life deeply, with intention, in each day's 10,000 encounters. Everything is *every thing*. Just as we awaken to full awareness in sitting still, so too can we be fully aware at any given moment of our breath and whatever else is in front of our nose. Tying our shoelaces as if for the first time . . . chopping vegetables on the out-breaths . . . folding laundry with care for the neat symmetries of layers of fabric. Conscious breathing in full awareness of eating makes mindful meals of everyday breakfast, lunch, and dinner.

Here's where the rubber meets the road. You might consider your daily activities as applications of the practice, yet they *are* the practice, in and of themselves — whether sweeping the porch or playing a guitar; answering a phone or driving a car; washing dishes and feeling the warm water, smelling the fresh detergent, and enjoying the circular motions, or just lazily pausing . . . breathing . . . smiling . . .

mindful walking

Slowly, slowly, step by step, each step
is a meditation, each step is a prayer.
MAHA GHOSANANDA

Formal sitting is traditionally followed by walking
meditation, particularly after a long sit. Time to stretch.
But walking meditation is meditation in and of itself.

Walking meditation is meditation walking.

Sitting meditation puts us back in touch with our
breath in our body. Walking meditation brings our body
in touch with our Mother Earth. (She's now 4.5 billion
years old. So why not celebrate?)

BASICS FOR BIPEDS

Here are the basic steps (pun intended):

1 Stand up. Pause — enjoy a couple of breaths.
   Smile.

2 Staying grounded in your awareness of breath,
   with your next breath, add walking.

3 Coordinate your steps to your breathing.

4 Step with your left foot, very slowly, for the duration of your in-breath, then step with your right foot during your out-breath, and so on. (So, rather than matching your breath to your steps, you're synchronizing your steps to your breath. *Ultra slow.*)

Be mindful of three aspects of walking:

1 Lifting your foot
2 Placing your foot
3 Planting your foot*

Flow with it. As natural as breathing is, so too can walking be a continual flow of motion, sensation, and awareness. As one foot sets down, the heel of the other foot starts to lift. Be aware of your breathing, your body following your breathing, and your smile.

Conscious breathing, mindful walking, joyous smiling — all become coordinated, in tandem, in mutual awakening. Slowly, slowly, step by step.

---

*Did you know that there are as many nerves (sensory "exteroceptors") in a human foot as a hand? One hundred thousand to two hundred thousand to be exact. And reflexologists map all our internal organs along our soles. To feel how vital are our feet to our well-being, all it takes is a good foot massage — or twenty minutes of walking meditation.

TEN TIPS FOR STEPS

> Move the way babies and toddlers move, without thinking,
> playfully seriously seeing what will happen.
> PATRICIA MUSHIM IKEDA

Meditation is never the same. (That's one reason it's so rewarding.) Walking meditation can be a keen reminder of this truth. While you grow familiar with it, here are some refinements of the basics. You can bring any one to mind anytime.

1 *Snail, ascending bit by bit . . . Mt. Fujiyama.* (Haiku, Kobayashi Issa.) When you take a step, it can be a very small step. Fractional. Maybe just a toe's length. After all, you don't dance with a partner to *get* anywhere; you're simply enjoying each moment together.

2 *Go as a river.* Feel the fluid interconnections of your tendons and limbs, muscles and nerves, mind and breath, steps and earth. With a group, notice how you might all fall in step with each other, like cells of one body, and honor that too.

3 *Equanimity.* Observe motion and rest, action and stillness, and your natural sense of balance, with equanimity. This also applies to the flow of perceptions, emotions, thoughts, and consciousness. It's all part of the dance.

4 *One breath. One step.* Can you be aware of this breath/this step — and nothing else? (No "next" step. No "next" breath.)

5 *How long?* As with sitting, give it twenty minutes. Try that at least twice. You'll know when a marvelous shift occurs.

6 *Where?* In a room or hallway. In a park, backyard, or up on the roof. In a circle or an oval. Traditionally, clockwise. With a group, start out with equal space between each person.

7 *Walk across a narrow, rickety, wooden suspension bridge — with hands free.* Hands and fingers can dangle down toward Mother Earth. Or, making a loose fist with one hand, place it in the center of your chest and clasp it gently with the other hand. Or join your palms together. See what feels right.

8 *Witnessing.* Set your gaze ahead and down, with soft eyes. Don't cling to anything. Let walking absorb your concentration. Effortless, it's a relaxed, open attentiveness. Forget labeling or evaluating. Don't know anything but be curious about everything.

    This can be on-the-ground training in inclusivity, evenly taking it all in.

9 *Notice what you notice.* Perhaps the freshness of air breathing in, its warmth breathing out . . . your half-smile . . . a mutual kiss shared by Mother Earth and the soles of your feet . . . the presence of group mates along the path, in tune with each other and nature . . . an ever-changing tapestry of perception . . . or nothing at all but walking in full awareness.

10 *Take a stand for universal peace.* All beings come from Mother Earth. Ourselves, included. Yet, for thousands of years, humans have imprinted upon her so much disharmony and violence. Mindful walking is a peace demonstration. Loving, mindful steps affirm a better world is possible, starting here.

IMAGES AND WORDS, WALKING

Walking meditation is an ideal occasion for Zen: choiceless awareness, open to whatever arises, without attachment. It's also a potent vehicle for focused meditation. Here are some amenities which might, from time to time, enhance your walking meditation.

Creative visualization can be integrated with breathing . . . stepping . . . smiling. You might visualize, with each step, a lotus blooming or a gentle, cool breeze blowing. You might imagine you're a lioness or lion. Or a queen or king, reclaiming your sovereignty, your footprints imprinting your seal. You might imagine you're an astronaut. After a long, long voyage weightless in outer space, you've safely reentered our atmosphere and now finally landed.

Thich Nhat Hanh suggests:

Give Mother Earth a massage with your feet.
Without her, life would not be possible.
In return, as we walk in mindfulness,
Mother Earth massages us through our feet.

Walking can be coordinated to a mantra or a prayer or a gatha. The word *mantra* (pronounced "montrah") is in common vocabulary now, as in "My manager's mantra is 'communication!'" The Sanskrit root means "protector of the mind-heart." It's a meditation practice unto itself whether you are sitting, walking, or just living 24/7. You might breathe and step to a sacred name or phrase. *Christ . . . Jesus. Hail . . . Mary. Have . . . mercy. Ha . . . shem. Sha . . . lom. La ilaha . . . illa Allah.* Reciting the name *Bud . . . dha* could affirm the human capacity for understanding. (The Sanskrit meaning of the root *budh* is "awake.") We are all capable of waking up.

Prayer works too. *Have . . . mercy. Give us . . . this day.*

All the mindfulness gathas begin with a conscious breathing mantra: *In . . . out.*) Mentally say *in . . . out* coordinated to your breath, your steps matching (left foot, *in*; right foot, *out*). Over the course of twenty minutes, you might apply the poem for Full Awareness of Breathing: *In, out / Deep, slow / Calm, ease / Smile, release / Present moment, wonderful moment.* Zen monk Phap Dang offers a simple, powerful practice: mentally saying "yes" with the in-breath, and "thank you" with the out-breath. One day, in walking meditation at the Green Gulch Farm Zen Center, gardener Wendy Johnson felt these eight words coming to her: *each . . . step . . . on . . . this . . . green . . . earth . . . brings . . . peace.* Spiritual teacher Ram Dass created a simple mantra which I also adore: *loving . . . awareness.*

You can always craft your own mindfulness blessing or vow, as need be. Here's one by me: *Breathing in, I renew my commitment* [in, *commitment*]; *breathing out, I practice surrender* [out, *surrender*]. And another: *Breathing in, I am grateful; breathing out, I am generous.* That's a good one for all seasons, not just economically uncertain ones. When we pause to consider the simple wonders of life, we realize how much there is to be grateful for. The expansiveness of gratitude finds natural expression in generosity, beginning with ourselves. Don't skimp. Don't be stingy with your life. When we think we have next to nothing, sharing whatever we do have (our time, our peaceful presence) loosens our heartstrings and liberates our mind. Such an attitude of openness nourishes our sense of abundance and resilience.

Remind yourself that we are an expression of the generosity and genius of Mother Earth. Walking meditation can thus be our expression of gratitude. Created by Mother Earth, we still carry her within us. She is not external to us, nor do we live outside of her. Walking meditation can thus be supreme prayer.

FORMAL AND INFORMAL WALKING MEDITATION

Formal walking meditation takes a flip in attention, coordinating steps to breathing. On the other hand, informal walking meditation measures breathing by our steps. Here's how.

Walking along in everyday life, we can still practice conscious breathing. (Why not?) Slow your pace just a tad, then count how many steps your in-breath takes and how many steps for your out-breath. Say, for instance, it takes three steps for *in* and three steps for *out*. Follow that measure as you walk. Soon you'll find your breathing, your steps, and your beautiful smile merging in refreshing, awakening body-mindful awareness. Over time, you might discern your out-breath has lengthened. Then you might count three and four, or three and five, or four and six. Find your own good average.

Informal walking meditation lets you continue mindfulness in public without drawing attention. Be anonymous. Be an urban Taoist. And consider that everyone else on the street is practicing walking meditation too, each in their own way.

I slow my steps an extra beat before entering a large building. I pause and set my intention to be aware of the unknown suffering contained within a hospital's walls . . . the low-key dramas of an airport's comings and goings . . . the multiple attentions of university students walking, bicycling, and skateboarding past . . . shoppers not always watching where they're wheeling their carts.

Once, at an airport, I saw a man in a trench coat hastening toward Gate 53 with his ticket in his mouth, pulling his luggage with both hands. Suddenly, I noticed something fall. I was walking slowly enough to pick it up: it was his wallet. I was holding it out for him as he noticed — *Uh-oh, wallet missing!* — looked around, saw it, snatched it out of my hand like a blue jay grabbing a peanut, and hurried on to Gate 53. There but for mindfulness go you or I.

Once you've experienced formal walking meditation you can draw from your well with just a few mindful steps. You can always walk mindfully amid a few moments of downtime. At a bus stop. In the kitchen, waiting for water to boil. Going from a car to a door. And, most informally of all, throughout your day, check in with how your feet are connecting to the earth.

THE PATH IS THE GOAL

> Take 5–10 minutes today to simply walk outside
> without any direction or purpose. Feel the
> freedom and miracle of being alive and on this
> earth. Take your time and walk slowly.
> KENLEY NEUFELD

I've learned to be mindful of where I'm going by awakening to where I am. For instance, walking home from the grocery store I often need to remember to pause and breathe. Otherwise I may already be shelving my stuff in my mind's eye while I'm still walking, thinking about work, mentally composing email, and so on. Pausing, becoming aware of my breathing in coordination with my steps, I then smile to be out and about beneath the cheery blue hue of the sky all around, punctuated with watercolor-strokes of clouds, the uneven levels of the pavement beneath the hill, and the whole dance of life.

The shift is from walking toward some unseen destination — as if I'm *marching*, marching into the future like a train on tracks — to a feeling of "Here I am, on my way," each step part of an endlessly unfolding pilgrimage. Thich Nhat Hanh, World Champion of Walking Meditation,* phrases this shift quite well:

> Because we do not set ourselves a goal for a particular destination we don't need to worry or hurry. Because there is nothing for us to get. Therefore walking meditation is not the means, but an end by itself. So each step that you take must make you happy, peaceful, and serene. Each step brings you back to the present moment. Which is the only moment in which you can be alive. . . . Each step is life; each step is peace and joy. That is why we don't have to hurry. That is why we slow down. . . . Thus we smile while we are walking.

---

*There are numerous books on sitting meditation, but his book *The Long Road Turns to Joy* is the first full-length manual devoted to walking meditation.

WALK WITH ME

At my tender age, (*gosh!* — seventy), I can regard my past as if it were a doll's house. It's as if I can lift the roof off, peer within, and see all the different rooms, some of which weren't clear to me then, or I'm only now seeing how one would inevitably lead to another or where I went after I'd zigged instead of zagged. And I consider how I used to walk. Looking back at myself as a tween (no longer a child, not yet a teen), I now recognize that somehow I'd identified "being in a hurry" as good. Looking back now, it feels like arrogance, like feeling "special." Yet, there I was, at school or on the street, marching instead of walking, two beats faster than everyone else. I proudly developed soccer-like moves for zooming around and ahead of people without slowing my stride. I never realized how this only set me apart from others, reinforcing an unspoken sense of isolation and quiet despair. Me vs. the world. (The winner: no one.) Sometimes, today, I still feel terribly hemmed in when walking in a crowd. When I do, I pause, noticing the arising of claustrophobia, return to my breath, deep and slow, and enjoy mindful steps.

Recently, I was reminded of the nature of mind when a regular in my mindfulness practice group brought a newcomer. She later told me she'd felt her friend needed it. Sure enough, I could soon sense in my bones how her friend just wasn't comfortable sitting quietly in silence. Then, outdoors on the grass, at Aquatic Park, we began our regular slow-walking meditation around a small stand of colossal poplar trees, overlooking waves softly breaking on a public shore. After a few steps, she stopped, turned to me, and wailed: "If I'm not busy doing something, I just can't do it!" Then she turned away and stomped off to her car, her car keys in her hand jingling like her jangled mind. Upon reflection, I realized this business of busyness has been true for me, in my own way. I think it is so for others too. It can be hard enough to merely fully inhabit our own skin, right where we are. At least she was able to consciously experience the human predicament and articulate it, perhaps for the first time. That awakening alone could mark a triumphant breakthrough.

When I first discovered walking meditation, I breathed a great sigh of relief — no more hurries, no more worries, able to live in the real world without my mind-made shackles, an ordinary human being stepping into freedom.

IT'S DIFFERENT FOR EVERY BODY

Through my Zen mindfulness practice group, I get to learn from others. We sit, walk, and talk about any recent experience. A woman from France was visiting us for a few weeks and said walking meditation felt to her like dancing. Hearing that, I realized I'd never put it that way before but that it's true for me too. Walking meditation can flow like tai chi, each motion leading gracefully into the next, in embodied, graceful flow.

She was a guest of Abe. Ninety years young, he's been a vital part of our circle for six years now. I remember one morning, after walking meditation, he shared with us how stepping on fallen leaves reminded him of past journeys . . . in New England, where maples turn amber . . . Korea, where he served in the Army . . . his childhood in the Bronx . . . yet all the while staying in the present.

Once, upon being introduced to walking meditation, a man a little younger than me, clearly moved, shared his impressions by smiling, pausing, breathing for a few moments, and then saying very humbly, gratefully, and selflessly, "Walking meditation reminds me how my body still fully knows how to do this, before there was a *me*." Clearly, it opened up a connection to healing, internal work he'd already been doing.

I also remember one gal telling us how chilly the dew felt, walking barefoot on the grass, yet how warm dew was in the sun — each felt different, both pleasurable. What a vivid illustration of equanimity! Comparing my life and its possibilities with the experiences of others, I am constantly fascinated at how others' stories are about myself too. I continually take refuge in how life reveals herself in myriad manifestations.

Step by step.

Breath by breath.

doing this deal on a daily basis
making it your own

Mindfulness needn't be yet another new chunk of *stuff* to try to fit into a day's schedule, alongside everything else. Gradually taking on meditation — in tandem with the bedrock support of an ethical lifestyle and in conjunction with the liberating insights of a wisdom tradition — can eventually be life-changing. Awakening mindfulness can permeate our lives like a morning mist that, after we've gone for a stroll at dawn, has saturated the fabric of our coats and sweaters, without our noticing.

Mindfulness holds a single truth with multiple meanings. For some, meditation is enough. A member of the Zen mindfulness practice group I host has been coming just for sitting meditation then leaving, for over a year now, so it must be beneficial for him. Meditation can confer marvelous, vital takeaways, such as less stress, sharper focus, higher productivity, better relationships, healthier habits, and so on. Noticeable results can become an incentive to dive deeper. At some point any positive outcomes become "extra" — it's the practice itself so many people love.

When I began, mindfulness was a point of reference. Later, it became my point of view. Now it's my life path. A path of simple, everyday reverence. I hope your own inner path will appear before you. Slowly, slowly, step by step.

Q&A

Q *What's the best meditation?*

A There is no best meditation. There's only your meditation, in each instance of it. As my grandmother used to say, "Get started and keep at it." One milestone is when you meditate without any thought of meditation.

Q *How do I know how long to meditate for?*

A You can practice PBS in as little as fifty seconds. Pausing, smiling, and enjoying ten breaths is a great meditation. Some notice how five or ten minutes a day makes a noticeable difference. (Regularity counts.) Twenty to forty minutes is a benchmark for formal meditation. You can measure a sit with a stick of incense or a meditation timer. That said, try sitting until you feel like you no longer wish to stop. It's like a kite that has taken hold in the sky and doesn't want to come down.

Q *Sometimes I just can't bring myself to stop and just sit. I try, but I get too restless. What then?*

A Good question. Please recognize how it's natural to feel distraction, even resistance. Next time, smile at it. It's important to gently invite *within* meditation a loving awareness of our straying and even obstinate mind and its hardwired resistances because meditation includes our experience in its entirety. It all fits. Sometimes, we need to become familiar with the One Who Just Can't Rest in order to connect with the One Who Is Not Busy.

Q *This is all well and good, sir, but what if I don't have enough time for meditation?*

A Well, my friend, if you think you don't have enough time, this might be a wake-up call to reexamine your priorities. Reevaluate your values. Things that matter most ought never to be at the mercy of things that matter least.

Time is all we have!

Life is like being placed on a vast blank scroll that unrolls as we continue to write and paint our lives upon it. When we stop writing and painting, it's done. Until then, there's always just enough.

Q *Dwelling in the present moment, is there development?*

A Great question! Is being in the now all there is? Well, along with life's ebb and flow, evolution is also taking place. Within the lazy aimlessness of life, there's also transformation. In the holy darkness of the earth, a seed is learning to become a flower. Flowers, in turn, give birth to further seeds of change. So awakening mindfulness could be seen as a form of heart gardening.

smile

WHAT'S HAPPENING? And, amidst all of this, who are you? (Who are you, *really*?) Meditation, in and of itself, may not fully answer this question. Nor may a positive lifestyle, alone. The key underlying lifestyle and meditation is *worldview*.

Everyone partakes of a worldview. Unexamined, it might be a hand-me-down, from family, peer group, workplace, society, ideology, or the winds of prevailing trends. Such unconscious frames of reference are like water is to a fish, invisible. But being unconscious of our views can cause needless suffering, as when they lead a driver the wrong way down a one-way street. (I call this Car-Crash Awakening.) Fortunately, awakening mindfulness comes with a wisdom tradition that can show us the Way.

Through meditation we contemplate what's really going on, inside ourselves, outside ourselves, and in the relationships between the two. Awareness of relationality gives rise to a mindful lifestyle, so as to minimize harm and maximize happiness. Yet meditation and good deeds aren't necessarily enough to free us. Awakened wisdom can.

As we'll see, three truths are intertwined at the roots of an enlightened worldview: (1) impermanence, (2) interconnection, and (3) selflessness. In a word, the Big Picture. Oftentimes, when we wake up from the little maze we mistake for reality and see the Big Picture, we just have to smile. Sometimes what began with anxiety and fear might end in laughter. It's always such a *joy* to wake up!

smile, life's not always what you think

Mindfulness teacher Ajahn Sumedho reminds us, "Whatever we think we are, that's not who we are." Life goes on, regardless. Don't take it personally. So why not smile?

In the next sections there's cause for further smiling as we look at what wisdom is, and isn't. Then I'll present three marks of reality for your wisdom eye to recognize. They're your PBS reality check. When you observe them clearly, you can tell you're in touch with reality. These each have practical applications. I'll also locate some common pitfalls to watch out for and, after a word or two on insight, I'll pause and review our journey.

WHAT'S SO WISE ABOUT A SMILE?

Awakened wisdom can seem ephemeral, elusive, like pollen. So sometimes just a smile can communicate it best. Here's partly why.

Mindfulness is becoming popular thanks to Western science. Yet it also draws from ancient Eastern wisdom traditions. As the two fields converge, there are gaps. Consider, for instance, the mind-body connection. No problem for Chinese and other Eastern cultures where the word for physical heart and spiritual mind are the same. But Western science has been following a dualistic worldview. Scientific research, for instance, is divided into a dualism of objective and subjective. Objective is good, and subjective is considered separate and unscientific. They ignore that we ourselves are both the object and subject of our studies. So, up to now, Western scientists have struggled to match up physical experiences and mental ones. This can be like asking, "How do we know if the light in the refrigerator really goes out when we shut the door?" Best maybe to just smile.

A smile reminds us that there's more to life than concepts and words. A smile relaxes our armor and lets us accept what's difficult. A simple smile affirms our intelligent alertness, our discerning curiosity, so we can see for ourselves, through direct experience. A smile can be an act of recognition, and understanding. And a smile can be a sign that what we're seeking (such as happiness) often doesn't need to be attained: it's already present. So a smile can both shine a light on our research trail and serve as our diploma. (Remember, awakening is lifelong learning.)

I don't worry about Western science. Having trained in Eastern worldviews and wisdom traditions for most of my life, I'm just waiting for it to catch up. Slowly, slowly, step by step.

WHAT THE BLEEP DO WE KNOW?

Some know wisdom through philosophy. The roots of the word philosophy mean "love of wisdom": *philo* = "love," and *sophia* = "wisdom." Such wisdom is often personified as feminine. Yet for centuries Western philosophers have seemed like lonely bachelors, rationalizing their unrequited love. They overthink their way to the Beloved. I sometimes think even mediocre mystics are happier than they are. (By the way, originally *mediocre* just meant "midway up the mountain.")

Analysis is important. But, to look clearly at life, we need to get past overreliance on faulty thinking, such as dualist view, and relying on the head without the heart. So many of us go about the daily affairs of living while lost in thought — mistaking our mental constructs and interpretations for reality. We're like the blind people in the famous parable. It's an old story, worth repeating.

Once upon a time, a village of blind people heard that something called an elephant had come to the next town. So they travelled there to find out what it was. One blind villager, feeling a leg, said, "An elephant is clearly a column!" Another blind person, feeling the tail, contradicted, "No, no, an elephant is a kind of rope!" Meanwhile, a blind person feeling the side of the elephant disagreed with both of them, saying an elephant is a leathery wall. Another blind person, meanwhile, feeling one of the elephant's ears, argued that an elephant is actually a fan, made perhaps of a large, thick palm leaf. Facing the elephant head-on, one blind person touching a tusk insisted an elephant is a spear and quarreled with the person alongside who was feeling the trunk and said an elephant is really a kind of hose.

The story illustrates how each of us goes through life clinging to our own personal "elephant." So all of us need to see clearly. (And, because there are real elephants, if we're not careful, we could get stomped on.) The story also invites us all to ask, "Have I considered what filters and concepts, expectations and projections make up *my* 'elephant'?"

Please compare that ancient parable with reports of contemporary scientists. We're informed that our galaxy is but one of hundreds of billions of other galaxies visible to our human eye. Moreover, one recent theory holds that 96 percent of the entire universe is "dark" — invisible to us. So the visible portion, such as atoms and galaxies, may make up only 4 percent of the cosmos. (Stay tuned: scientific views are subject to change.)

But that's not all. Within the visible portion of the universe, we only perceive less than 1 percent of the electromagnetic spectrum (radio waves, microwaves, radiation) — although birds and bees see the ultraviolet spectrum that we don't. What we hear is less than 1 percent of the acoustic spectrum — although dogs, dolphins, and bats hear more than we do. We're like frogs at the bottom of a well, thinking the few stars we see are the whole night sky. From an outlook based on limited, mistaken perception, we practice various forms of deception. We fool ourselves and each other, and, in so doing, deny ourselves our highest capacities. How good, then, that with mindfulness comes a wisdom tradition offering us time-tested remedies for our inborn blind spots.

what is wisdom?

The word *wisdom*, like the word *ethics*, might seem off-putting. Perhaps it might evoke daunting, lofty concepts chiseled in stone high atop colossal, fluted columns of a library, courthouse, or university — Truth . . . Honor . . . Fidelity . . . Justice — a bit intimidating if only because we have to crane our necks just to read the words, not to mention living up to them. Yet, thanks to meditation, seeing clearly, we can continually find truth everywhere. Since truth extends through material reality and beyond, and includes us, ultimate wisdom might be only pointed at: a bigger picture that resists our tendency to try to pin down and "thingify" everything. Yet wisdom's truth is hardly any *thing* at all. It's so ungraspable that the wisdom teacher in Ecclesiastes tells us "everything is a mere fume of a vapor." (Ecclesiastes 1:2. Translation, GG).

Awakened wisdom is not so much a product as a process: a way of seeing and being and doing. There's a Chinese word (慧, *hui*) for an active sense of wisdom worth considering. On the bottom half, we see a heart, which is also "mind" in Chinese. Above, is a figure with two parts: two bunches of branches and below them a grasping hand; together they form a "broom," to "sweep." Rather than wisdom being an accumulated body of *knowledge*, this is a way of *knowing*.* So we see wisdom can mean clearing our mind, purifying our heart, clearing away, emptying, to be open to whatever's at hand. It's not a thing but an activity, as open and as ordinary as sweeping a porch, and no less useful.

Wisdom. (On the left, in ancient style. In the middle, standard style. On the right, a more flowing, cursive rendition.)

This clarity can be liberating. We're no longer running after pleasure, nor running away from pain, nor running to hide from our dissatisfaction at always running around and around in circles. Sweeping away afflictive thoughts and emotions and thoughts that block our path, our heart is free to sing. We get out of our own way. Aware of just what is happening, as it is happening, we can cultivate a mindfulness that trains us to be freely open

---

*The origin of the word Zen (*dhyana*, Sanskrit; *jhana*, Pali) is akin to the Greek root *gnosis*, "knowing." For some, it's silent knowing. For others, it's a Not Knowing (agnosticism). One could also say it's *understanding*. However it comes to you, chances are it's borne on a smile.

to life and our heart. Such peace and calm, courage and equanimity, insight and wisdom have been sought after for millennia, by rulers and armies. And they're ours to enjoy if we just pause, breathe . . . and smile.

three marks of reality

Wisdom is a vast ocean. We learn from it wave by wave. When from time to time we awaken, we realize: we *are* the ocean, as well as its waves. To nourish your awakening, you might consider just a few highly potent drops from the ocean of wisdom:

> Flow (impermanence)
> Interbeing (interconnection)
> Openness (selflessness)

So simple, this bears repeating.
Everything is:

> Provisional
> Permeable
> Pregnant with possibility

Imagine such words as *those* carved over colossal doorways of hallowed institutions!

Please note: just two or three drops of the nectar of awakened wisdom are powerful enough to liberate your world.

SEE FOR YOURSELF

Don't take my word for it. Test awakening wisdom for yourself. Pause, breathe, and see:

1 Breath (like life) is as *impermanent* as morning dew. With your next breath, please notice how the previous breath is now done. Gone. Linger in this awareness. Everything changes. Notice too how impermanence allows breath to be breath. Ever flowing. Otherwise, we'd be frozen in time, like statues. (Long live impermanence!)

2 Everything is *interconnected*. Beginning with your next breath, please notice how breath (like life) is interconnected. There's no in-breath without an out-breath. And vice-versa. Notice too how breath acts as a hinge between body and mind-heart. Breath conditions our heart and mind and body; heart and mind and body condition breath . . . deep . . . slow . . . easy . . . calm. Smile!

3 Notice how breath (like life) is *selfless*. Free. There's no ownership, no personal stake attached. No abiding selfhood of its own to burden or enslave us. To grok this, simply *wait* for the next breath.

No expectations. This is like being an ancient
hunter in the forest, who becomes as still as
the forest, waiting for the deer. Let yourself feel
surprise and awe when a "next" breath comes, of
itself, *selflessly*. Let breath breathe itself

Notice too the space between inhales and
exhales: no breath. As open to possibility as
the sky is vast. Mind the gap: this spaciousness,
no thing whatsoever . . . utter blankness . . .
unlimited potential. Let this *openness* be like an
ungraspable ground underlying all breath, the
way silence supports all sounds, as you note how
unique each breath is.

Take a vacation from maintaining an identity
all the time. Be only breath.

Our spiritual ancestors have given us a wisdom tradition. We now have a chance to study, observe, and realize
its true meaning. Such awakened wisdom isn't remote or
abstract. It's first person. Real time. Just devoting loving
attention to our breathing we tap into wisdom in action.
This is real and this is happening. And this is scientific.
Here's an experimental process that's empirical, replicable
under average conditions, verifiable through experience
and observation. With that in mind, here's a primer
about three characteristics of reality, open gateways of
awakening wisdom in any situation. If we don't see the
whole elephant yet, we can see these footprints. We're on
the path.

flow
wakening from the illusion of permanence

What is the most rigorous law of our being?
Growth. No smallest atom of our moral, mental,
or physical structure can stand still a year.
It grows — it must grow; nothing can prevent it.

MARK TWAIN

Who says "forever"? Everyone and everything we know
and encounter is bound to change.

Everything and everyone.

All the more reason to let go of intangible concepts
and insistent cravings. Understanding how *momentary*
life really is — ours to be lived only moment to moment
— is the dawn of awakening wisdom.

BECOME INTIMATE WITH CHANGE

Make change your friend. After all, one reason for practice is because life is impermanent. To develop a healthy
relationship, journaling can be a trusty ally. List daily
encounters with impermanence, no matter big or small,
profound or insignificant. Beside each one, record your
attitude — positive, neutral, or negative. Our attitudes
shape our world.

List where you find yourself opening to flow and how that feels and where you tend to get stuck and how that feels. Can you find gratitude for an obstacle as an opportunity to work your way through it? See where your experiences of being comfortably open to flow in some situations might be replicable in other situations; extrapolate creatively. Remember: our attitudes toward impermanence may hold us back, but impermanence lets our attitudes change.

Pause . . . breathe . . . smile. You can always connect with impermanence, and your attitude toward it, through awareness of your present-moment breath. No PhD required. Complex algorithms and the ultra-precise tweezers of science will never really compete with the incredible instrument of being human. Our intuitive mindfulness is capable of incredibly keen discernment of how subtly our sensations, feelings, and thoughts arise and fall away, as does our breath, manifesting and vanishing like bubbles on a pond. Just like that!

Growing aware of impermanence, you might encounter one kind of obstacle I call a Case of Mistaken Identity. All too often, we *identify* ourselves with pleasures that are only temporary. So often we get lost in an endless parade of enjoyments — superfluous merchandise . . . escapist entertainment . . . spectator sports . . . mindless eating . . . keeping up with a fashion "look." Is this who we really are? Instead, we can recognize and relax our ingrained tendency to crave, to hang on to our cravings, and to identify ourselves with them (or our dislikes, which are just cravings' flipside). Hanging on can lead to hang-ups. It's true all across the board. Even a luminous, blissful state of mindfulness is impermanent. What timeless truths we may think we possess today may later be revealed as but a line of letters traced in foam at the water's edge. Nothing can be really satisfactory if we're clinging to it. Awareness of impermanence reminds us to step watchfully through life openhanded, openminded, openhearted. Smiling.

It is said that life is high school with money. Well, whatever grade level you're at, you can earn a diploma by learning the most important single lesson I know: how to let go.

THE ART OF LETTING GO: HONOR THE RESISTANCE

Anything which is troubling you, anything which is irritating you, THAT is your teacher.

AJAHN CHAH

Letting go teaches us to locate our resistances to change. As obvious as it may seem, no one can let go and hold on at the same time. So by learning to yield we learn about where we're still holding back, noting constrictions and blocks that still persist.

Change is as constant as the sun coming up each morning: not a problem, in and of itself. It's a fact of nature. Yet it's a fact of *human nature* that we resist accepting this is so. For instance, it's natural to die; it's human nature not to accept this. We think death only happens to other people, not us. Fortunately, most of us don't have to take death head-on, right away. There are plenty of other resistances to use as grist for the mill. After all, what we resist, persists.

Training your capacity for insight, you might enlist your journal and record your negative or problematic attitudes toward change. For a month, say, list common resistances: where you don't go with the flow but pull back instead and withhold your energy. If this is a problem, there could be a tension you feel in a certain situation at work. (Where do you feel it in your body?) Or you might hear an inner critic who passes judgment while you're working on a project or building a new relationship. (Whose voice does it sound like?) Explore the causes and conditions that are associated with resistances. Certain words can be triggers. Outdated senses of reality, or self-image, might be at the root. The values of others might get internalized as your own, without question. Mental or emotional investments may no longer be rewarding. (Divesting and changing them may not be as difficult as recognizing them in the first place.) And you might not be the cause at all. You might feel resistance in encounters with other people who've not yet awakened to their own baggage.

Meditation can be your laboratory of further research and discovery. After grounding and stabilizing, coming home to your body in the present moment, explore when resistance arises in consciousness, and what would be at stake if you were to let it go. Actually, meditation itself is good training in observing resistance firsthand and working with it. You might recognize when you sit down to be still how the mind might want to get busy instead, erecting fences against boundless freedom. (What's up with that?) Regard how much time and energy you've invested in resistances and how much time and energy gets freed up when they're released.

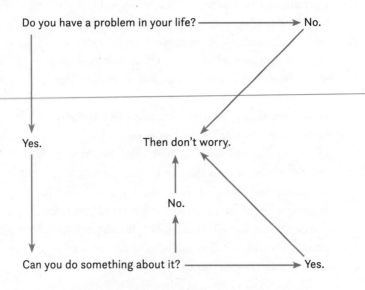

Do you have a problem in your life? ⟶ No.

Yes.

Then don't worry.

No.

Can you do something about it? ⟶ Yes.

Worrying doesn't change anything — letting go of worry can.

This is a different way. You're not fighting resistance, nor beating yourself up over it. Rather, you're honoring it for teaching you about yourself and what it means to be human. Our vulnerabilities can point out to us how we are inherently good at heart, just as we are, and locate where we need to pay attention, look deeply, and take care so we don't give up on our highest aspirations. Instead of gnashing your teeth the next time you encounter change that seems not for the best, recall the mindful way: greet change as an opportunity to study, observe, practice. When good news arrives, say, "Thank you." But when bad news arrives, honor the resistance, and say, "Thank you."

USING RESISTANCES TO BUILD RESILIENCE

> The secret of living a meaningful and fulfilling
> life is to be ready — at every moment — to give up
> who you are for what you could become.
> BRIAN GOODWIN

In our fast-paced society, it's not uncommon to reinvent a career time and again. It takes resilience to be able to adapt to whatever's around the corner. Resilience is a virtue anywhere, actually. Plans change. Stuff happens. Sometimes our obstacles can knock us down. Resilience enables us to get up, honor the resistance, dust ourselves off, and move on, learning as we go. We come to realize any creative lifestyle implies occasional failure. It comes with the terrain of life's peaks and valleys. Irish playwright-novelist Samuel Beckett put it this way: "Ever tried. Ever failed. No matter. Try again. Fail again. Fail better."

Because mindful living trains your observation of impermanence in daily life, when impermanence comes upon you in a big way it won't be such a shock since you're already working with it. You can connect with your vulnerability and embrace your feelings, summon your inner calm, and practice resilience. Over the long term, challenges may not necessarily get smaller, but you can learn to handle them with more spaciousness and equanimity, clarity, and a smile. When life throws you another chance to learn and grow, you do your best and let go of the rest.

The goal is seeing things more clearly, as they are. When, *shazam!*, I see a flash of lightning, I can appreciate it just as it is, without sighing, "Oh, darn! Here I was going to have a garden dinner party!" And, precisely because it is impermanent, listening to thunder I smile and savor every syllable. As I become more resilient, I become an epicurean of impermanence.

interbeing
wakening from the illusion of separateness

To develop a complete mind, study the science of art,
study the art of science. Learn how to see.
Realize that everything connects to everything else.
LEONARDO DA VINCI

Have you heard the word *interbeing*? It's a wisdom
practice that I embrace in every moment, in every
encounter. If I'm sitting by a tree, I contemplate a
leaf on a branch. I can see in it the soil below me, the
passing clouds that shed gentle rain, the sun feeding
the world its radiant energies, and the vast atmosphere
within which we breathe together. So, looking deeply,
smiling, I can recognize the whole cosmos is present in
this leaf.

I can also put it this way: the leaf is composed of
nonleaf elements. These elements inter-*are*. Say I were
to remove the water from the leaf, it would instantly
collapse. The leaf *is* because the water *is*. The same is
true for each of its elements. *This* is because *that* is.
To be is to inter-be. My heart opens wide: interbeing
strengthens the compassion that impermanence gives
rise to, revealing how interconnected everything and

everyone really is. Why is it important to understand this? Because it can liberate us from the illusion of separateness, so we can wake up.

Practical and theoretical examples of interbeing are as numerous as stars in the skies and sand on the shores. Interbeing is what enables pausing breathing smiling to interdepend upon each other. For instance, the insights that our worldview nourishes are confirmed in our mindful contemplation and intentional action. Interbeing also informs our Full Awareness of Breathing. My awareness grows full as I feel the interbeing of breathing: the air in my lungs and the air around me intermingle effortlessly. My awareness grows fuller still as I feel my body and my breath and my mind conditioning each other. And in our healthy lifestyle, when we identify with other beings as closely as we do ourselves, the wisdom of interbeing is present right there too: it's the recognition of nondifference between "us" and "them."

We might have had a mystic inkling of this when we were young. As adults, we still can sense the truth of interconnection. We speak of "the web of life," for example. Yet, when we appreciate this with the heart, there's a shift in how it *feels*. Physician Albert Schweitzer calls this feeling "reverence for life." Years later, Thich Nhat Hanh coined the term *interbeing*. Influenced by him, Reverend Martin Luther King, Jr., eloquently invoked it when he referred to the way the universe is structured as "an inescapable network of mutuality." So it's wonderful, if not surprising, how contemporary systems theorists from diverse fields are now all coming to view life, at various levels of scale, in terms of a self-creating process that can be called interbeing. It brings me a smile to think of the day when *interbeing* is in every dictionary on the planet.

OLD AND NEW AGREE: EVERYTHING IS INTERTWINGLED

Stop me if you've already heard of Indra's net. Indra lives in a heavenly abode. His palace is on sacred Mount Meru, the center of all realms. Thanks to some cunning craftsperson, over his palace is a net that stretches infinitely in all directions of the cosmos. (In fact, this net *is* the cosmos.) The net itself has no independent, isolated existence. It's a network of a series of interconnected meshes, and each mesh has its place and responsibility in relation to the other meshes. Now, because Indra has highly refined tastes, this net is made of precious jewels, of infinite number. They sparkle like stars in the sky. Now, here's the kicker. Were you to inspect just one jewel up close, in its pristine surface you'd see all the other sparkling jewels, infinite in number. But wait — that's not all. Look very steadily and you will see *each* of the gems reflected in this one gem is *also* reflecting all the other gems. And so on, ad infinitum. This infinite process models the limitless, unimpeded interpenetration of all things.

SYSTEMS THINKING

> We are participants in a dynamic whole
> within which we define ourselves and create our reality
> through our participation in relationships.
>
> DANIEL CHRISTIAN WAHL

The worldview of Indra's net spreads like pollen. For
instance, it provides a useful working metaphor for
modern Western scientists seeking to describe many
new findings that didn't fit their given worldview.
For centuries, Western science had been breaking
down the universe into *parts*, and the parts into
subparts — each labeled by its own specialist. And
seldom would specialists converse with anyone outside
their turf. Lately, however, to see the whole elephant,
scientists have been adopting interdisciplinary, *systems*
approaches that consider the relationships as well
as the parts. Indra's net provides one framework for
what science is just beginning to learn about complex
networks, whether they be our ecosphere, interactions
of atomic particles, thoughts within the brain, social
networks, city planning, and so on. Physicist and
ecologist Fritjof Capra notes, for example, that sugar
is sweet, but its components — carbon, hydrogen, and
oxygen atoms — aren't themselves sweet. The sweet-
ness is in how they interact in a network of bonds
— and how that network interacts with the chemistry
of our taste buds.

This more holistic view is often called "systems thinking." For example, if you think of your relationship to each of this book's three parts, and their relationship to each other, that framework is systems thinking. Systems thinking takes us beyond piecemeal tactics, such as making spreadsheets for a linear accounting of problems and solutions, with a percentage allowance for possible unintended consequences. Systems thinking considers the full-spectrum impact of all functions as interrelated. Wise financial investors, for example, are applying systems thinking. They think of ROI (return on investment) in terms of a triple bottom line, profit-planet-people. Aligning economics within life's regenerative essence (rather than vice-versa), they're changing the world and economics at the same time.

New and old agree. If I may be permitted, I invite you to consider the Native American view, which frames the range of our responsibility, at any given time, in terms of seven generations of our ancestors who've brought us to this moment and seven generations of our descendants down the line whom our deeds in this moment will influence. The succinct eloquence of filmmaker Ted Perry gets the last word here:

> Humankind has not woven the web of life.
> We are but one thread within it. Whatever we
> do to the web, we do to ourselves. All things
> are bound together. All things connect.

WELCOME TO THE HOLOGRAM

A neat aspect of the web worldview is that any part contains the whole. *Every* thing is everything. For instance, any slice of consciousness contains the whole universe. One working model of Indra's net can be found in a form of photography called holography. Holography uses laser light to record and project in 3D. Imagine, say, a skateboard in midair. Shining a laser into a hologram of it would make the image appear in midair, 3D — made out of light. (You could walk around it and see that this was so.)

Now here's the twist. If you were to snip off just a tiny corner of the hologram, then project just that fractional bit with a laser, you'd still see the full 3D image (only slightly less vivid). The information about the whole image is distributed equally throughout the sheet of film. Every iota contains the whole. So some scientists now speak of the structure of the universe as holographic. Neuroscientist Karl Pribram and physicist David Bohm speculated that our brain is a holographic storage system. This is mind-boggling science. For the rest of us, the good news of interbeing is that we're never cut off from the light of wisdom inherent in life. Even the simplest truth can contain the most cosmic. And we're never really alone.

Feeling isolated can be damaging. Contemporary activist philosopher Charles Eisenstein reminds us: "We are not just a skin-encapsulated ego, a soul encased in flesh. We are each other and we are the world."

Going one step further, maybe human beings are lenses through which the universe contemplates herself — and vice versa. It may not constitute an official job description, but sometimes I find it a really good focus on sanity.

NO GARBAGE, NO ROSES

> Suffering is not enough . . . you need to smile to your sorrow because you are more than your sorrow.
> THICH NHAT HANH

This is *because* that is.

Here's a practical application. Consider a rose. Looking deeply, we see a rose is made of nonrose elements: water, air, soil, and sun. Plus compost. If you don't garden, you may not know it's common to recycle organic waste (compost) as mulch to nourish the soil. Now, please look deeper. Like the smelly garbage that nourishes the fragrant rose, we can see our suffering as mulch for our thriving.

We see the Art of Happiness also consists of the Art of Suffering. They inter-are. Like mulch and roses, our pain and our joy are one. So we might select a place for pain in our heart's garden. We know that it will come with reactive attitudes of fear or rage, but we can recognize that as needless suffering: night soil to use for mulch. Pausing allows us to remember not to push away or run away from difficult emotions. Avoidance or aversion just complicates the situation, only adding further negative energy into the equation, like trying to put out a fire with gasoline. Instead of turning away, we can recognize, embrace, understand, and transform a difficult emotion when it arises, rather than feeling trapped, a victim. In a kind of alchemy, the negative charge of suffering transforms into wholesome energy.

Straight out of the yucky mud blooms the pristine lotus.

No mud, no lotus.

Studying facets of impermanence while appreciating the dynamic nondualism of interbeing can beautifully expand and enrich our worldview as to how these two

This is because *that* is. There is light in the dark, and vice-versa. They define each other. They inter-are.

deep insights affect our own lives. This could be enough. Yet, sooner or later, those twin drops of wisdom nectar could also lead to a third — one that can be a supreme mind opener/heart widener/life liberator, plus an excellent reason for a smile: nonself. It's not as daunting as it may sound. You could also call it openness.

openness / nonself
wakening from the illusion of selfhood

If we look deeply, we find that we do not have a separate self-identity, a self that does not include sun and wind, earth and water, creatures and plants, and one another.

JOAN HALIFAX ROSHI

Thich Nhat Hanh once smiled to confess that, early in his studies, he'd read about nonself, and it seemed too abstract to him, until, *aha!*, one day, he got it. Impermanence views reality through *time*. Everything changes. So in terms of *space*, not a single thing anywhere possesses any fixed, constant, abiding identity. No "self." Interbeing seals the deal. A rose's selfhood is water, air, sun, and soil, of which it's made with no separate identity outside of them. Take away just one of those elements, and there is no rose. And, as with all created things, so it is too with the nature of the self.

Tasting this drop of wisdom nectar in meditation, we can feel firsthand what it's like to dwell beyond a constricted sense of self, in pure possibility. Meditation shows us how life is available more fully once we get out of our own way. A virtuous lifestyle lets us enjoy this openness while in society, not blindly following unevolved habits and whims of our ego nor stepping on each other's toes. And a wise worldview encompassing nonself finds everyday life so much more intimate, spacious, and free.

This can be very practical. For example, given this impersonal, selfless nature of reality, we needn't take everything personally. Or, driving in traffic, I don't honk my horn because it looks like that driver up ahead just cut me off. I realize they just took a left and smile at my reactive mind. I smile as I remind myself that I am not my last mistake. I can stop beating myself over the head about the past, and move on. I don't have to identify. In a word, recognizing nonself helps keep me sane.

Any serious, practical investigation into reality must include the nature of self. Here follow some prompts for your own possible points of inquisitive departure.

SHOW ME YOUR MIND

Have you paused to consider how you think of self? For instance, when your self is suffering, could you show me your self so I might heal it? Can't find it?

No self —

— no problem.

Pure awareness is selfless, without locality and without limits. Yet our culture's traditional concepts of self often play variations of the skin-encapsulated ego. Self is thus imagined as a miniature version of ourselves, dwelling within. Browsing my parents' bookshelves, I remember a science textbook I happened upon when I was seven, which represented that worldview. I can still visualize its drawings of a faceless person, meant to be Little Me, sitting in an executive chair, in a nondescript gray room inside my head, monitoring my bodily systems through a desktop screen, issuing orders from a phone connected to an internal public-address system.

Yet, in fact, there's no fixed, separate self, distinctly isolated like a pigeon-stained statue in a park. Cognitive scientists cannot find any location for the self, any more than a surgeon can point with a scalpel to where the soul resides. They view self, rather, as an unstable construct, continually born of shifting interchanges of physiology and environment, in the given conditions and encounters of any moment. It might be more correct to speak in terms of selves. Frankly, in my humble opinion, I think we have as many selves as there are moments of experience. Freeing ourselves of a problematic and fundamentally illusory notion of self, through coming to know nonself, is reawakening to our true nature, our inherently light and happy heart, our deep soul.

> My glasses . . . do not belong to me or to you,
> or they belong to all of us. But they know about my
> tired old eyes, and so they let me use them.
>
> SHUNRYU SUZUKI

One fun way to recognize nonself is noting its ownerlessness. Do you *have* a self? (Or, are you possessed by your sense of self?) Consider our thoughts and feelings and sensations. They usually come to us without our deciding to think or feel or perceive them. Yet, the minute they appear, *bingo!*, our ego claims ownership. They're now *my* thoughts, *my* feelings, *my* sensations. This includes owning emotional problems, as if they're our personal baggage. Yet, in actuality, I don't decide to feel chilly or think of my sister or wish my mind to wander. These just happen, of themselves.

We might explore this phenomenon further. A physicist, say, might understand nonself through the general theory of relativity ($E=MC^2$). Time, space, and matter are a continuum. Interdependent, the parts thus have no separate identity. And neither do we.

Consider our memory of ourselves, as if it were a photograph. A photo is a picture *of* something — a cloud, say. Does the photographer now own this cloud that once was? Similarly, consider our awareness, consciousness. It too is always conscious *of* something: a rose, a rock, a baseball bat. But there's no independent self that *owns* the consciousness of the experience. Mindfulness enables us to disengage from the identification process so as to experience directly and immediately. Awareness can be given the chance to be simply aware, in and of itself.

Existence and our experience of it is in constant flux. A photograph (and a memory) is a vivid souvenir of a moment that's gone. So too the self can be seen as an afterimage (and also a bulletin board of predictions). We might also consider how interdependent reality is. So our consciousness is as much a part of the cloud of which we're aware, as the cloud is an integral part of our consciousness. They inter-are. Neither the subject nor the object of consciousness has an independent self. "I" am "that."

As with any mark of reality, the realization of nonself can be as easy and as immediate as paying attention to breathing. Right now, just pause and, at your next inhalation, consider: whose breath is *this*? This air might contain oxygen produced from plankton in Borneo, carried by planet-encircling winds. This air might contain atoms previously breathed by nameless ancestors . . . and yet to be breathed by descendants still to come.

Is this in-breath "your" air because your own lungs are drawing it in? (Does a chimney own its smoke?) Is an exhalation "your" air because it comes from way inside of you? So have you patented it yet? Copyrighted it? Have you planted your multicolored flag upon it yet, colonized it in the name of your king and queen? Has your corporation branded it with a logo and a barcode? Does it have a website and a Facebook page?

And, after exhaling, what about that brief, blank portion? (Mind the gap!) That space of no breath exists very much without any selfhood. Zero. All of reality is suffused with such limitless, groundless spaciousness with which we can grow appreciatively intimate: the vast, blank, open, fertile void, enabling anything to be possible. Totally free. Selfless.

SELFLESSNESS: THE ULTIMATE IDENTITY

Volumes have been written about self, selfhood, overself, nonself. However we frame it, our sense of self has become ingrained over many thousands of years, so changing it takes time. Yet it's empowering to realize we can do this. Mindfulness studies the nature of self, in one's own self, by one's self. Self-study: life-long learning. A mindful way is to learn to empty ourselves of conceptions and biases. Then we can understand self through a practical program of interacting with other selves with intentional virtue (pause), meditation on the nature of reality (breathe), and a wisdom tradition of insights (smile). Wisdom sees awakened mind as being as innately empty as a bell, as luminous as a star. Meditation is a chance to enjoy that reality, like strolling through a forest in the moonlight without bumping into any trees. Ethics guides us in living this way with others, seeing that they are just like us.

This is so cool. Since this clarity is intrinsic to our nature, there's no need to spend the rest of your life cross-legged atop a steep, craggy mountain (as in the typical cartoon stereotype of meditation). You don't have to shave your head or give away all your needless stuff to the poor (even though some people might still harbor a nagging suspicion deep down that they really ought to). Just pausing to breathe, smile, and let go of anything extraneous to our innate, self-luminous awareness can be a sublime fifty-second clearing.

Simple.

Sitting in choiceless awareness . . . bare attention . . . naked presence . . . is, in and of itself, selflessness in action. So too can guided meditation, visualization, and mantra be following selflessness as motivation. For a further boost, you might pause midway during meditation and ask yourself, "Who is meditating?" (I cannot answer that one for you.)

When peeling the layers of an onion, we find there's nothing at the center. So too is reality ultimately empty, even of any single center. Selfless. Open. Fortunately, such a nonself nature of things is not a negative downer but, rather, a wellspring of creativity. The sky's the limit. A bowl is so, only because it's empty. Having seen the light, we can harness its flame so we can cook our grains, greens, beans — and onions.

Let's conclude our tour of selflessness with sound meditation and then what has viably become a primary practice for some: socially engaged practice.

SOUND MEDITATION: EARS WIDE OPEN

One ubiquitous object for contemplation of selflessness is space. Typically, we tend to focus on objects. Instead, gaze for a bit at the space all around things. Anywhere. Carrying this further, lying on your back and contemplating a clear blue sky is a magnificent way to connect with the blank, open selflessness of your ultimate identity. (All the rest is weather.)

Another ever-present object of focus is sound. Sound meditation is as easy as pie. Just sit still . . . and listen. Be one big ear.

What's closest? Can you hear a slight ringing in your ears? If so, contemplate that faint drone. Next, tune in to your breath. (A slight adjustment inside your nostrils can make it audible.) You're not *doing* anything, just listening.

Next locate any scattered, midrange sounds, and contemplate them as well. Then include distant sounds — becoming aware of the vast spaciousness of silence, through which all sounds float.

As you experience all this, let go of the ego's habit of categorizing experience. Don't let Little Me label some things as noise and others as sounds, or even identify them. Just listen to all you're hearing as a special kind of avant-garde music all its own. Enjoy the flow of these ambient sounds as a spontaneous, contemporary, present-moment, free music concert, full of unique rhythms, melodies, harmonies, pitches, and timbres. Savor, as you listen and contemplate this overlooked yet ever-present, ever-unfolding, fascinating sonic festival celebrating ordinary life.

Stay with it. Continue just being one big ear.

Next contemplate how pervasive is this acoustic field, stretching in all directions. (No inner vs. outer. A hiccup and a car backfiring are all sound.) A soundscape without limit. Sounds and the silence around them are equally part of your mind. They *are* your consciousness, and your consciousness is all of *this*. No separation.

Still enjoying the unfolding concert, simply accept the recognition that everything you're hearing is you, yet also a reflection of nonself. This is true. You aren't willing any of these sound events into being . . . the sound of breath . . . the wind through the trees . . . the whoosh of traffic . . . someone's stomach rumbling (never mind whose). Sounds are always going on, within us and around us, without us — on their own.

Because you're hearing them, they're all a part of you. They're an integral part of your mind. Yet they're also all "non-you" (since "you" are composed of non-you elements). Totally selfless.

Ninety-nine percent unrehearsed, life is a performance. Enjoy this unrepeatable improvisation thanks to the selflessness of life. There's no liner notes to distract you, nor a conductor nor a score. As with your awareness of it, there's no beginning, no middle, no end. People come in, leave for a snack, and come back, as they please. Wherever you are, yours is the best seat in the house.

ENGAGEMENT IN THE WORLD

If you think of mindfulness as only a quiet, wordless state of contemplation, please think again. Engaging the world in creative, life-affirming ways can be a perfect balance of self and nonself, as mindfulness in action. Engaged practice flies on balanced, twin wings of wisdom and compassion. Encountering the wisdom of impermanence engenders tender compassion. Applying that compassion toward ourselves and the world, as one, is "engagement." Inner and outer transformation are not separate. Practicing this nondual wisdom precipitates insight into how self and world are not separate, but are a process of mutual dependence, arousing still yet more compassion. Selfless motivation was touched upon in our survey of intentionality. Now we consider how a capacity for limitless kindness can be realized, made real, by being put into action. Otherwise, compassion can be mere empty words, a hollow gesture, a snowflake.

Question: What are you doing for others? Self-care and care for our world are the same, just differently viewed through various pairs of eyes. Change the names, and the stories of others are about us. For instance, volunteering at a local hospital, if not hospice, we come face-to-face with impermanence, and our own attitudes toward it. Benefiting others, caregiving also opens us up to our own strengths and fears, giving our heart a healthy massage. Coming to grips with the nature of suffering in everyday life is good training in resilience, intuitive insight, and awakening. Ideally, it can be true charity, which means selfless giving without concept of recipient, giver, and gift. Give it a try.

Case in point: when I began volunteering at my local Zen hospice, I'd expected I'd first be given an orientation lesson or training materials. But, no. Two staff members met me in the hall, sincerely thanking me for my commitment as they calmly ushered me into a bare room where a gaunt, white-haired man in pajamas lay under covers on a big bed — dying — and, closing the door quietly behind them, left me there. Sitting down at his bedside, silently breathing, alone together, the insight suddenly arose that what this person needed most wasn't for me to utter comforting words or ask probing, profound questions or any of that — only for me to just be present. Face-to-face with impermanence, together. So I let go of my preconceptions and simply offered my humble, sincere presence. And, from that moment on, I knew — that was exactly what was needed of me at the hospice from here on out.

Call it on-the-job training. Awakening the mind of love, on the spot. Aware of the temporary nature of everything and everyone, anyone might find themselves falling open, facing the silent power of authentic presence. This vulnerability can nurture insights that are totally personal, utterly universal, and absolutely invaluable

Engaged spirituality has roots in many creeds. Christians might see Jesus in each patient, each doctor, each visitor. Jews might be practicing good deeds (*mitzvoth*) to repair a broken world (*tikkun*). Muslims might be fulfilling their vow to manifest what the One has instilled in them as a force for good. Some might nourish the deep roots of their human nature in the elemental forces of Mother Nature. Others could be observing the Golden Rule. It's up to each person. Through engagement with the world, we can observe firsthand how happiness is not solely an individual matter: we're all in this together.

I correspond regularly with a prisoner. Some of my friends facilitate meditation within prisons. People who've done this over the years have noted their presence can inspire a consciousness of awakening in not just prisoners, but also officers and administrators; they too want to be peaceful and happy. A smile of kindfulness ripples. This is how systemic change occurs, person by person. Systems are composed of people. And we are all interconnected.

As we awaken peace in ourselves, we awaken peace in the world.

Awakening peace in the world, we awaken peace in ourselves.

Socially engaged spirituality doesn't take being Gandhi or Joanna Macy, Vine Deloria, or Martin Luther King, Dorothy Day or Thich Nhat Hanh.* Just notice and

---

*During the American war in Vietnam, Thich Nhat Hanh and others established a school to train thousands of young people, monks, and nuns who were doing social service in poor villages as spiritual practice. He coined the phrase "engaged Buddhism," but the trend was already present. Such Buddhism isn't bound by monastery walls but rather is engaged in the world at large as well as within one's self, as one.

engage whatever difficulty or sorrow in the world captures your attention in a deep way. Whatever it is: addiction and recovery, child abuse, community awareness, disease, ecosystems, food security, forgiveness, genocide, the homeless, inequity, poverty, refugees, restorative justice, trauma, and so on. (Each intersects all the others.) If we happen to notice any particular one, it must reflect something within ourselves that resonates with it. Lessening needless suffering in the world can promote a lessening of our own needless suffering, and vice-versa. The inner and the outer are interconnected. Naturally, you'll find yourself joined by others, in mutual support.

Journaling, we can note our responses to woeful or hopeful personal events and world events, both interconnected by the same theme. We can set aside time in our meditation, when calm and stable, to recognize and understand the roots of suffering there that concern us and consider how to transform them — and the roots of hope that inspire us and consider how to amplify them — in ourselves and in the world.

Help create the world that you want to live in and that you want your great-great-grandchildren to live in.

Next up, I'll point out some detours to watch out for. We'll also see how insight links up to awakening wisdom. Then we'll take a step back and review.

lanterns for travelers
tips about traps

Whether you're a newcomer to mindfulness or a veteran, here are some tips about traps into which many a tiger has fallen (in addition to my "spiritual bypassing" as manifest on a crowded bus):

"Self" destruction
Gaining mind
Attachment to form

May these friendly travel alerts keep you from stubbing a toe on stones hidden along the Path.

"SELF" DESTRUCTION: DON'T LOSE YOUR EGO

There's a popular misconception that meditation means erasing our ego. Careful: don't get frozen in an ice cave of selflessness. I've seen some folks dedicate themselves to ego eradication with a vengeance. But this can be like throwing the baby out with the bathwater. Sure, in reality, self may be a survival mechanism, a virtual-reality arcade, a fiction, but it can be a convenient fiction, nevertheless.

Many an awakened mystic still remembers their zip code. We need a healthy ego to navigate through life's myriad choice points. It's like being aware of what temperature is best for baking a cake, plus sensing when the stove is too hot to touch. Similarly, learning to live without being dominated by desire or bias, we also learn to cultivate curiosity, discernment, and heartful analysis.

We just need to decenter so we're not always reacting to everything as if the whole world revolves around the Little Me. Extreme forms of self-absorption manifest as narcissism or workaholism, self-cherishing or self-pity. Self-denial can take the form of indifference, asceticism, anorexia, and so on. Both, at bottom, are equally self-centered. So we learn to always seek a middle path.

WATCH OUT FOR GAINING MIND

In some mindfulness circles, there's an expression for focusing on ends rather than means. It's called "gaining mind," or thinking only in terms of what's to be gained.

True, seeking benefits brings many of us to the practice in the first place. Over time, however, this could nourish a limiting, mistaken, dualistic mindset: if I do *this*, then I will get *that*. That dualism also reinforces the plight of the skin-encapsulated ego, imagining good things await us in a world "out there" (somewhere), and which we ("inside here") lack and thus crave. Our practice is, instead, of awakening to how our true nature is already completely adequate, just as it is.

It's wonderful to practice mindfulness *as is*, just to do so, in and of itself. Then, any benefits are a welcome byproduct of our creative diligence, organic, rather than a brass ring on a merry-go-round off over the rainbow.

Instead of grasping at mindfulness as if it's a tool to gain a desired result — it's ultimately far more rewarding to consider it as a way. There is no way to mindfulness. Mindfulness is the way.

This bears a bit of expansion. In the fifth century, the traveling teacher known as Koheloth asked, "What's our *gain*, what remains after all our work? — hard work at which we toil under the sun?" (Ecclesiastes 1:3, emphasis added). His question still resonates today. How can we protect our seed intention of awakening from being tainted by our inclination of predicting profit, calculating our gains? Our inherent tendency to think of what's in it for us, what we can get out if it, instantly adds shopping carts by the entrance to our heart, with scales for weighing at check-out counters, accepting cash, checks, credit cards, cryptocurrency, and so on.

Japan has a word for the remedy, *mushotoku*. It means "without looking for personal profit or gain." It's a good intention for practicing mindfulness: for its own sake. It's also an excellent philosophy of life. No expectations. Do it just to do it. No attachment to any outcome. We're entitled to the work, but not the fruits. The least hair's width of a calculative mind considering profit or gain can be another form of self-absorption, which will only feed a deluded outlook and unhappy outcomes.

Ultimately, there may be no thing at all to be gained — but consider what you might lose: anger, anxiety, confusion, depression, distress, envy, fear, and so on — plus unsatisfied expectations ("I" = expectations). You may be pleasantly surprised when mindfulness awakens you in ways you'd never even expected.

DON'T GET ATTACHED TO FORM

One more unfruitful habit where freelance mystics can get bogged down is attachment to form.

It's good to find a middle way between regular, formal traditions and always practicing on the fly. Obviously we need some discipline. But it's possible to become so filled with names and forms that there's no room left for receiving fresh insight. Of course, it's easy to fall back on a habit, rather than keeping things new each time. Please consider this analogy. Imagine there's a person who needs to get across a river. They gather branches and build a raft. The raft ferries them to the other shore. But then they carry their raft around with them, rather than park it at the shore before moving on.

Don't do anything because it is so; do it to make it so.
Stay creative.
Make it new!

what is insight?

If meditation is about being, and ethics is about doing — we might say wisdom is about seeing. I hear an example of this when people say they understand something by saying, "I see!" I mention this because we'll round out our wisdom tour with a spotlight on the clear seeing known as insight.

When we're in touch with the way things are, we see clearly. We can look deeply into ourselves and into life itself. Such seeing is insight. As practiced in mindfulness, this process is best described as flying balanced on two wings, stability and penetrative seeing. I like to think of it as going from *Ah!* to *Aha!*. From calm solidity *Ah!*, we can apply the lens of impermanence, interbeing, and self-lessness to our sensations, feelings, and thoughts, to see clearly and look deeply for penetrative insight *Aha!* into whatever's going on.

Fortunately, such insight is not occult or arcane. We don't need a crystal ball to see it. Mindfulness gives us space for the chance of insight to take place of its own accord. When we're acting responsibly and have a solid, stable base in mindful awareness and a clear conscience, we're just naturally prone to seeing clearly, looking deeply, and feeling out what needs to be done. From an authentic, existential foundation — genuine, intimate insights can intelligently arise. Insights can arise in the same manner as thoughts, feelings, and sensations. We can observe them as they occur — just as we observe our breath — openly, without clinging. To become an insight adept, just pause breathe smile: pause when you sense the opportunity for insight to arise, breathe into the situation, see clearly, look deeply, and smile at seeing familiar things in new ways.

One way insight gives us new eyes is in allowing us to recognize our *attitudes* about reality along with our experience of it. Why is this important? Our attitudes shape our experience. They act as colored lenses through which we filter reality. Vietnamese mindfulness teacher Thich Vien Ngo sums up his philosophy in eight words: "Happiness or suffering is a matter of perspective." True enough. Sometimes our apparent problems are not really the problem. The problem can be in a false perspective of which we're unconscious. So our insights into our attitudes can liberate us from much needless suffering.

Insights are everyday portals to timeless wisdom. In them, we can see the universal in the personal through direct experience. Witnessing the aloe vera blossoming in my garden, any theories of growth and regeneration merely confirm what I'm already seeing. Insight might be spontaneously realizing something important that reconnects us to the bigger picture and to our heart. Insight might let our intuition feel out what's ahead and around the corner in a skillful, relational way. We might apply insight for creative problem-solving. It's often used in dealing with tricky or difficult emotional or mental issues. If we notice that a difficult feeling or thought keeps popping up, we can circle back later intentionally to practice mere recognition of it. In a stable state of sitting or walking meditation, we can pause to look clearly into its presence in our landscape. What might have been an area of constriction, an obstacle, or a difficulty can be transformed through healing insight.

Mindfulness is not an art of judging or suppressing our feelings and attitudes, an art at which everyone is already an expert. Mindfulness is rather a delicate art of experiencing feelings and attitudes, first and foremost, as is, without anything extra. It's thus a skillful way of recognizing and understanding them without identifying with any as being our true self. We master the art of being aware of our sensations, feelings, and mental formations — as they arise, manifest, and pass away — as plainly as we see breath does. It's a practice of "mere recognition": appreciating and accepting our experiences with a gentle matter-of-factness, without identifying ourselves with them or building a narrative around them with *me* at the center.

As with our actions, mindfulness gives our thoughts and feelings enough space so we can respond heartfully rather than blindly react, and thus grow and become free. When we encounter life's impermanence (flow), and interconnection (interbeing), and selflessness (openness) — we learn to recognize our attitudes toward them. Unaware of life's impermanence we might fall into depression, perhaps by mistaking fleeting pleasures for lasting happiness. Or awareness of impermanence might strengthen our resilience and durability, while engendering our compassion for the fragility of all things, ourselves included. When we experience any moment's interdependence with other moments, as well as with people and things, we could feel confusion, even paranoia. Or this fact might stimulate our equanimity and care, gratitude and generosity, and a sense of personal responsibility. As gardeners of the heart, we can carefully discern which attitudes are wholesome and worth cultivating and which are weeds, requiring us to see into their roots in order to clear the ground.

Because these three marks of reality inherently pertain to all things — including our body, feelings, and mind — insights are always available to our mindful awareness. Experiencing life directly and touching life deeply, we can access truths about life only found in life itself. Flowers of insightful worldview flourish in our heart's garden when watered by the clear mind of consistent meditation practice, watched over by the clear conscience of a positive lifestyle, and tended in harmony with the changing seasons. Our flowers teach us how to be beautiful with what we already have, to grow, and to be free.

THE MIRACLE OF AWAKENING

> A half-smile is the fruit of awareness and joyful peace of mind, and it also nurtures and preserves that awareness and peaceful joy. It is truly miraculous.
> THICH NHAT HANH

To be open to selflessness, interbeing, and flow is to experience reality directly. What a liberating and beautiful marvel! Seeing clearly, everywhere we look there are miracles. In his poem "Miracles," American mystic bard Walt Whitman has confessed:

I know nothing else but miracles . . .
  . . . the exquisite delicate thin curve of the new
      moon in spring [is a miracle] . . .
  . . . every hour of the light and dark is a miracle,
  Every cubic inch of space is a miracle.

The miracles of life, without need of conceptual filters or abstract verbal analysis, are right in front of us right here, right now, to be lived, head on, just as they are, and just as we are. Another name for this freedom of selflessness is "nirvana." Thich Nhat Hanh advises us not to wait until we die to see it. It might be too late. The kingdom of heaven is now . . . or never.

wisdom wrap-up

Awakening, we find no secret laws waiting to be blindly obeyed. There's no "right" answer to life's endless riddles, only *your* answers . . . how you go about the great matter of life and death . . . awakening to your part in it all . . . the real work. Every day. One day at a time.

VERSES FOR WISDOM MEDITATION
Having toured a wise worldview, here's a set of parallel lines for immediate encouragement and possible long-term training:

Breathing in, I'm aware   [in]
    I'm breathing in.
Breathing out, I'm aware   [out]
    I'm breathing out.

Breathing in, I'm aware   [impermanence]
    of the impermanence
    of my breath.
Breathing out, I smile at   [smile]
    the impermanence
    of my breath.

Breathing in, I'm aware   [interconnectedness]
    of the interconnectedness
    of my breath.
Breathing out, I smile   [smile]
    at the interconnectedness
    of my breath.

Breathing in, I'm aware   [selflessness]
    of the selflessness
    of my breath.
Breathing out, I smile   [smile]
    at the selflessness
    of my breath.

Giving five minutes to each verse yields a twenty-minute formal meditation, but this works informally too. For example, when you're in the midst of stress or difficult emotions, return to your breath. Perceive how changeable breath is, as are all things too, including ideas and identities, emotions and stress. If you're feeling isolated, abandoned, or worthless, see if you can bring your awareness to your breath, survey how connected it is to the universe, as you are too, belonging, perfectly at home right here in the company of all of creation. Feeling stuck, be conscious of your breath and enjoy how naturally and freely it flows, without the need for control.

To sum up, just as we saw awakened wisdom through life-giving breath, so too can we explore it through water, the precious blood of our planet. Sleepwalking, we're like fish in an artificial goldfish bowl on a shelf; when we awaken, there's the great ocean of reality for us to swim in.

Impermanence reminds us that the ocean is ever changing. Endlessly in flux. Never the same. It is as poet Charles Reznikoff puts it: "The ceaseless weaving of the uneven water."

Interbeing reveals that the sea is a collection of water drops (one is all), containing rain and snow and dew and salt and fish — and the whole ocean is inherent in just a drop (all is one), full and complete.

Selflessness informs us that neither an ocean nor a drop reveal any separate, fixed, permanent identity. Nor do they need to. Neither the ocean nor its waves need to search for their own wateriness in order to splash huge wide kisses upon a shore. They just do.

Buoyed up by the vast, deep waters of wisdom cruising along on its perpetual waves of insight, we find we are as fluid as the water encircling the planet and circulating inside of us. We are embedded in a cosmos where earth, water, fire, and air are ever transforming each other. We *are* this. And we're capable of being aware of it as it's occurring. Here is a font of living wisdom beyond any *concept* of wisdom.

All the rest is commentary — as is this wordless poem by my first Zen teacher, Paul Reps:

> wave   wave   wave
> but down below
> no come   no go.

Q&A

Q *I think I get impermanence and interbeing. But I'm still struggling with nonself. What's your advice?*

A   Notice how stubborn self is, that it puts up a struggle when questioned. (Does it feel threatened? Is it issuing ultimatums?)

Please consider: what (and where) is this self, so attached to you that it might fear being let go of?

Anyhoo — no worries. Nonself is really part of our true nature. If you're keeping a solid lifestyle and contemplative practice, then by looking deeply at impermanence alone, related marks of reality become clearer in time.

Q *Can you say a little more about wisdom and action in everyday life?*

A Certainly. When insight arises and illuminates how things really are, compassion naturally arises, and this is an invitation to action. Considering impermanence, for example, we realize how we'd thought it would all go on forever. Now we recognize we'll eventually have to part with all that is near and dear to us — our family, our friends, even our own body. And, being aware of life's precious, fleeting nature, how can we not feel compassion for ourselves and others? Naturally, we then want to act accordingly.

So wisdom and action go together. Everyday wisdom is realized in everyday action.

Remember, our knowledge isn't timeless, absolute truth. Ground your understanding in your own life. As economist and philosopher Nassim Nicholas Taleb says, "What I learned on my own I still remember." Then insights into impermanence, relationality, intention, and selflessness won't be concepts but everyday realities.

We're not striving to reach some intellectual or conceptual plane of being or to awaken in some remote celestial abode. Instead, we're seeing our ordinary lives as the playing field where the game of awakening can play out. After all, everyday life is our daily address.

Q *Pausing for setting intention — and breathing as meditation — no problem. Now that you've laid out this wisdom angle, too, how do I know if I'm viewing it right? (Besides by smiling.)*

A Moving the frame from "me" to "we" can be a good basis for a wise worldview. It's also equally good for a beneficial lifestyle and contemplative practice. For example, you might consider practicing mindfulness in community as well as at home. Besides mindful sitting and walking, there's talking. Practicing deep listening and speaking from the heart together, communicating about our understanding of mindfulness in our daily lives, builds supportive, loving community. Sharing your practice with others, you'll find insightful checks and balances. Practicing in community has been likened to boiling a bunch of potatoes in a big pot: as they knock against each other, they smooth out each other's bumps and rough spots. And there's also the wonderful mutual support that enables us to trust in the human family and in our capacity to wake up. Author Mirabai Starr reminds us, "Waking up is a community affair."

But why wait? You might also consider how we're always in community, all around and within . . . aminos, bugs, birds, bacteria, enzymes, flowers, people, stones, and the sun and moon. We're always in relation. Truth is everywhere.

Q *So then how much is being in community a part of the practice?*

A It's not a part of the practice, my friend. It's really the whole of the practice.

Smile

END COMMENTARY

WHAT IS MINDFULNESS? One translation of the Sanskrit word for mindfulness is "remembering." Remember. Come back. This is your life. This is the only life you've got. So mindful awakening might be also called "remindfulness."

Remember: this is not the dress rehearsal.

This is it!

the art of awakening

Awakening can be gradual and sudden. Formal and informal. Personal and transpersonal. Brief, or lifelong. And it's an art, like music and painting, yoga and cooking, medicine and dance, and love. And, like all arts, it takes practice, plus a sense of play.

At the outset, artists often begin by imitating what they're drawn to, until they find their own voice. Ninety-nine percent of us need models. Sometimes, on foggy nights, we need a finger to point out where the moon is. But a finger pointing at the moon is not the moon. Meaning, don't cling to a helpful finger or be distracted if it wears a fancy ring or is decorated with a fascinating shade of nail polish. Don't forget the real work. In contemplation of the moon in the fog, we're seeing our own radiant, awakened, undying nature.

If you discover anything along the path that's nourishing, healing, transformative, by all means, use it. But please don't do so because you heard about it in the media or from a friend or in a book (even this one). Test it out in your own life. Then, if it proves beneficial, befriend it. Adopt it. Maybe even make it a small ceremony, a personal ritual like always putting your keys in the same place when you come home — second nature.

Make it sacred.

Make it your own.

the rest is up to you

I've presented awakening mindfulness here in a format handed down for millennia, as a three-fold way. Its three spheres overlap and interact in quite a variety of ways, so your practice is always a living ecosphere.

For example, connecting with our aspirations and our worldview is itself meditation. And they take form as deeds. Our deeds can serve as an impartial mirror. Thus we come to practice meditation in action. Knowing how we can act in right relation — to ourselves, to others, to our world — our path becomes free of obstruction.

We are freer to more fully devote attention to what's happening with a steady focus, a calm mind, and a clear conscience. Meditation is our ever-present base of refuge. We can always come home to our true nature — where we can hear our heart's silent songs.

And meditation can verify our insights and intentions, confirming them in the present moment.

Our practice of enduring moral values and timeless contemplation grows deep roots in ancient wisdom tradition, renewed by our own engagement. A selfless motivation enlarges our scope to become as wide as the sky. A nondual view enables us to see how our path itself becomes our goal. Step by step. We accept any occasion as an opportunity for awakening mindfulness . . . which is to say, living fully and freely, as we were meant to . . . in harmony with all that is. Moment to moment. All the time.

The keys are in your hands. They can open many doors, but it's up to you to go through. Or, as the cable car driver told me recently one morning on my way to work: "I've been blessed by The Best. He woke me up this morning and said, 'The rest is up to you.'"

pause breathe smile

THE TIME HAS COME for me to lay my pencil down. As
I do so, I invite you to join me in one last brief round
of pausing breathing smiling. (As you now know, in my
book, everything else is mere commentary.)

This time I'll invite you to review, with a few breaths
for each: . . . what's pausing? . . . what's breathing? . . .
what's smiling?

Settle in and ground yourself, in your body and your environment. Assume what describes for you a regal, relaxed
posture . . . of awakening, loving awareness. Come home
to yourself, arriving in the here and in the now.

As you feel yourself breathing, see if you can recognize
how such a little thing as pausing to prepare to sit, pausing
to be conscious, pausing to clear your mind, can change
your entire experience for the better. If you witness this,
explore your attitude toward pausing, allow yourself to
really feel it, whatever it may behold: relief, calm, satisfac-
tion, accomplishment, appreciation, kindness, love.

Next, see if you can flash immediately into full awareness . . . with just one breath. Breathe, and see. Maybe your concentration focuses automatically. Maybe you spontaneously enjoy your inhalation and exhalation in its entirety . . . a continuous sense of moment-to-moment awareness . . . as an unbroken circle.

Following your breathing, feel how your breath brings your awareness and your breathing body together . . . in a wordless wedding.

Savor whatever qualities of your breathing you notice and examine how discerning your awareness can be, in and of itself.

If one of the qualities you discern happens to resemble joy, nourish it. Gladden up. Invite a half-smile to be born upon your lips. And if you aren't feeling it, why not smile anyway — what have you got to lose?

Connect your awareness to your body and feelings and mind. With your next breath, look within. What's your internal weather report today? Feel how easily your mind can look deeply and see clearly.

At your next inhalation, see if any of these three aspects of reality come to mind of their own accord: flow/impermanence, interbeing/interconnectedness, selfless/openness. If any one presents itself, inhabit its space, connect with it, and appreciate how the seeds of wisdom you've been planting are already sprouting.

Give yourself a moment to take all this in. Pausing.
Breathing. Smiling. Let your heart dance. Let yourself
come alive.

Breathing in, be aware of your breath, your smile, the
present moment . . . and your awareness of them. (What
else could there be? This . . . is . . . it!)
    Breathing out, let go of any tension or heaviness . . .
in your body . . . your spirit . . . your soul.
    Feel your full awareness as no different than your
life . . . all of life . . . life itself.

Whenever you're ready, look anew at the light in life —
and love.

— Nothing different than how we began.
    A pause. A couple of conscious breaths. A half-smile.
So.
    So please continue at all costs . . . as you set this book
aside . . . as I set my pencil aside . . . and we go forth . . .
awakening . . .

Acknowledgments

I sincerely thank my publisher, Tami Simon, for following her dream and awakening millions thereby; my editor, Caroline Pincus, down-to-earth, with a well-tuned ear for my writing voice, plus a high-quality person to boot; Nancy Owen Barton, catalytic literary agent, canny editor, and fellow wayfarer; Leslie Brown, still point in a revolving world and always full of cheer; Chloé Prusiewicz and Lindsey Kennedy, both really wonderful and top-notch at marketing and publicity; Beth Skelley and Rachael Murray, no mere artists and designers but rather something more magical and alchemical; Jill Rogers, for an eagle eye and a steel-trap mind; Denise Nguyen, for her singing hand and silent joy; Charylu Roberts, O.Ruby Productions, for music engraving; and Ronny Schiff, for music editing.

Thank you to my dear siblings in the Plum Village Engaged Buddhism tradition; East Bay Meditation Center; Dragons Leap Meditation Center; the Honorable Frederick T. Courtright, for more than permissions; Mangalam Research Center, Ed Ng, Ron Purser, and Zachary Walsh for the retreat on Socially Engaged Mindfulness Interventions and the Promise of Making Refuge; Rich Fernandez, Brandon Rennels, and Linda A. Curtis for the Search Inside Yourself training; Dr. Jon Kabat-Zinn for the Kanbar Lecture at UCSF; Oscar Bermeo; Gillian Coote, Sydney Zen Centre; Amy Rennert; Nancy Fish, Parallax Press; Lim Kooi Fong, Buddhist Channel; Heidi Geyer, Browser Books;

Peter Levitt; Patrick Marks, Green Arcade Books; John Nguyen; Mark Nguyen; Steve Silberman; Swas Tan; Larry Ward; advance readers Marc Allen, John Bell, Steven R. Berger, Ben Carrall, Patti Deuter, Eduardo Drot de Gourville, Judih Weinstein Haggai, Rick Hanson, Rev. Ronald Kobata, Raymond Lipovsky, Gaetano Maida, Ted Meissner, Mitchell Rattner, Larry Yang, True Garden of Cypress (Chan Bach Uyen); the science experts, word experts, and writers community at Well.com, with special thanks to David Finacom and Jane Hirshfield.

To the Noble Eightfold Path, of which Pause Breathe Smile is a shorthand abridgement; The Mindfulness Education Group, with whom we happen to share the same three-word program title, Pause Breathe Smile, and an aspiration for a world where generosity, good will, and trust are viewed as the bedrock of peaceful, nurturing relations; Elizabeth Gilbert, who launched the three-word book title into perpetuity; Bill Murray, for his advice to his brother, echoed in the opening of "The Rest Is Up to You"; Shunryu Suzuki, who introduced the idea of our already being perfect and standing a bit of improvement; Alan Watts, who coined the phrase "skin-encapsulated ego"; John Welwood, transpersonal psychologist who coined the phrase "spiritual bypassing"; Shohaku Okumura, author of the expression "living by vow"; Ted Nelson, pioneer of computer networking, who developed "intertwingularity"; and Thich Nhat Hanh, who coined "interbeing," "Radio Non-Stop Talking," "keeping our appointment with life," "No mud, no lotus," and "Go as a river."

For Handy Reference

Please feel free to tear these pages out, or scan or print them. I invite you to keep it in a journal or on a bulletin board, in your pocket or purse, or as a bookmark. May it serve as your map, compass, and steering wheel.

AWAKENING MINDFULNESS

PBS is composed of just three parts. But water is made of just hydrogen and oxygen. A complex, resilient, regenerative system can emerge out of just a few components and their interrelationships. Here's a breakdown of the three PBS components for handy reference.

lifestyle (pause)

Definition   Conscious conduct, intention, motivation, relationality, values in action, ethics.

Examples   The Golden Rule, the Ten Commandments, the Five Mindfulness Trainings.

Mottoes   "Aware of the suffering . . ." "Do no harm." To your attention to self, add "and others." "Do unto others . . ." "Energy follows intention." "Middle path."

Practice   Mindfulness bell, mindfulness blessings, mindfulness trainings, journaling.

Reminders   Be conscious of the roots of your intentions and also acknowledge their impact on others.

Study. Observe. Practice.

contemplation (breathe)

Definition   Being still; being deep; grounding, centering; intuitive inquiry; first-person, present-moment attentiveness, with kindness, curiosity, and equanimity; letting go.

Examples   Zen (open awareness); or focused (such as guided).

Mottoes   "Clear your mind." "Be still and know." "Be the breath." "Pay attention." "Notice what you notice." "Loving awareness."

Practice   Anything is an opportunity. Daily practice is no different than your life. Formal and informal practice reinforce each other. Let the line between practice and nonpractice dissolve.

Study. Observe. Practice.

worldview (smile)

Definition   Looking deeply; clarity, insight, understanding, wisdom; harmony with What Is.

Examples   Impermanence, interbeing, selflessness.

Mottoes   "Not always so." "This is, because that is." "No self, no problem." "The ultimate point of view is that of no views."

Practice   From stability and calm, apply the lens of impermanence, interbeing, and selflessness to your awareness of your sensations, feelings, and thoughts. Journal.

Reminders   Avoid self-destruction and self-cherishing, "gaining" mind that calculates benefits, attachment to form, spiritual bypassing, and dualism. Understanding manifests as love in action.

Study. Observe. Practice.

SAMPLE SCHEDULE

Just for reference, here's one possible, full-fledged schedule (my own). Whatever you do, I hope you always keep your appointment: your appointment with life.

> Wisdom studies (ongoing, alone and in community)

> Mindfulness trainings (review every full moon, at minimum)

Meditation (four days a week)

Formal sit (twenty minutes or more, morning and evening)

Walking meditation (twenty minutes or more, such as before lunch)

Mindful meals

Practicing with a group (as often as weekly) — sit, walk, talk, study

Day of Mindfulness (weekly) — day or half-day of sitting, walking, mindful housework, mindful meals, studying, sharing, energy work, deep relaxation, journaling, and so on

Lazy days (weekly) — no formal plans, everything optional

Retreats (occasional) — because sometimes, in order to advance in our spiritual practice, we need to retreat

Keep your practice innovative and creative. Don't do it because it is so; do it to make it so. Make it new.

Rome wasn't built in a day. It takes ten years of study to become a chess grandmaster; even more to compose music really well. But time is all we have. What are you doing with the rest of your life? (Starting now)

Slowly, slowly, step by step.

PRACTICE COMMUNITIES
Every year, there are more and more communities of mindful living. A few are fairly large while others meet in people's homes. None of them knock on people's doors. For a directory of some with which I'm familiar, visit mindfulnessbell.org/directory.

If you've never meditated with a group, as an initial exposure you might consider visiting a Quaker meeting (Religious Society of Friends) just to sit with other people in silence, with the least degree of formality. If there's no Zen/mindfulness community nearby, please consider starting one of your own. I'd be more than glad to offer assistance in finding or setting one up. (Contact: Gary.Gach@gmail.com)

Permissions

The author is very grateful to Parallax Press for permission to republish the following: The Five Mindfulness Trainings, reprinted from *The Mindfulness Survival Kit: Five Essential Practices* (© 2014) by Thich Nhat Hanh; gathas on waking up, and turning the water on, from *Present Moment Wonderful Moment: Mindfulness Verses for Daily Living* (© 1990, 2006); a mindfulness meditation by Thich Nhat Hanh, beginning "Breathing in, I know I am breathing in," adapted from the Sutra on the Full Awareness of Breathing, reprinted from *Calm, Ease, Smile, Breathe* (© 2009), from which the poem "In, Out, Deep, Slow" is also taken; the song of the same name, from *Basket of Plums Songbook: Music in the Tradition of Thich Nhat Hanh* (© 2013), collected and arranged by Joseph Emet; and our opening epigraph by Sister Dang Nghiem, from *Mindfulness as Medicine: A Story of Healing Body and Spirit* (© 2015).

To Mayumi Oda, for her *Smile* from *Being Peace* by Thich Nhat Hanh, Parallax Press, © 1987 Mayumi Oda.

To Kathryn Hannan and Duncan Mackenzie for permission to republish the gatha in coloring book format by Christine Mackenzie.

Permission to republish *Untitled*, 1948, by Saul Steinberg (ink on paper, 14¼ x 11¼ in., Beinecke Rare

Book and Manuscript Library, Yale University), © The
Saul Steinberg Foundation/Artists Rights Society (ARS),
New York.

Special thanks to *Tricycle: A Buddhist Review*, where
a short portion of this book originally appeared in a
slightly different format.

The four intentions at the beginning of "Mindfulness
Trainings" are from "Practice: What Are My Intentions
for Today," by Sylvia Boorstein, *Lion's Roar*, November
2, 2017.

Every effort has been made to trace or contact copyright
holders. Any omissions or corrections in terms of
copyright will be gladly incorporated in future reprints
of this volume.

About the Author

Gary Gach's lifelong career is as a freelance writer and freelance mystic. That is, he's been writing formally since he was ten and meditating since he was eight. He teaches in the Plum Village tradition of Vietnamese Zen master Thich Nhat Hanh and has been facilitating a weekly practice group, Mindfulness Fellowship, in San Francisco for over ten years. A dynamic speaker, he's well regarded for keynotes and panels and for training and coaching individuals and groups.

With ten books to his name, his work has also been published in over one hundred periodicals, including the *Christian Science Monitor*, *Harvard Divinity Bulletin*, the Huffington Post, the *New Yorker*, *Lion's Roar*, Patheos, *Tricycle*, and *Yoga Journal*, and over a dozen anthologies such as *A Book of Luminous Things*; *Chicken Soup for the American Soul*; *Language for a New Century*; *Technicians of the Sacred*; and *Veterans of War, Veterans of Peace*. He's been honored with an American Book Award from the Before Columbus Foundation, a Nautilus Book Award, and a Northern California Book Award, and has been a recipient of grants from the Korean Literature Translation Institute and Lannan Foundation. He enjoys live music, haiku, and swimming the Bay. Visit him at GaryGach.com.

About Sounds True

Sounds True is a multimedia publisher whose mission is to inspire and support personal transformation and spiritual awakening. Founded in 1985 and located in Boulder, Colorado, we work with many of the leading spiritual teachers, thinkers, healers, and visionary artists of our time. We strive with every title to preserve the essential "living wisdom" of the author or artist. It is our goal to create products that not only provide information to a reader or listener, but that also embody the quality of a wisdom transmission.

For those seeking genuine transformation, Sounds True is your trusted partner. At SoundsTrue.com you will find a wealth of free resources to support your journey, including exclusive weekly audio interviews, free downloads, interactive learning tools, and other special savings on all our titles.

To learn more, please visit SoundsTrue.com/freegifts or call us toll-free at 800.333.9185.